BROKEN THEORY

BROKEN THEORY. Copyright © 2022 by Alan Sondheim. This work carries a Creative Commons BY-NC-SA 4.0 International license, which means that you are free to copy and redistribute the material in any medium or format, and you may also remix, transform, and build upon the material, as long as you clearly attribute the work to the authors and editors (but not in a way that suggests the authors or punctum books endorses you and your work), you do not use this work for commercial gain in any form whatsoever, and that for any remixing and transformation, you distribute your rebuild under the same license. http://creativecommons.org/licenses/by-nc-sa/4.0/

First edition published in 2022 by Uitgeverij
An imprint of punctum books, Earth, Milky Way
https://www.punctumbooks.com

ISBN-13: 978-1-68571-048-4 (print)
ISBN-13: 978-1-68571-049-1 (ePDF)
DOI: 10.53288/0393.1.00
LCCN: 2022936486
Library of Congress Cataloging Data is available from the Library of Congress

Book design: Vincent W.J. van Gerven Oei
Cover image: Alan Sondheim

spontaneous acts of scholarly combustion

ALAN SONDHEIM

Broken Theory

:

Contents

Preface   9
Maria Damon

+++ +++ +++

Broken Theory   13

+++ +++ +++

"Shuddering, I Write":
Interview with Alan Sondheim   207
Ryan Whyte

For Azure Carter

Preface

Alan Sondheim's opening is logical, methodically putting one foot in front of the next, where "foot" is "keyword." A resonant word in the final sentence of each paragraph becomes the opening focus of the following paragraph. This is a procedure anyone can follow. It both previews and belies what comes next: a methodical but chaotic whirlwind of pulsating anxieties and sensations girded in verbal detritus that is one big Achilles heel, one big, ornately wrought, beautiful announcement of vulnerability.

What follows is fragmentary and ambitious. Each fragment is part of an archipelago of thought, seemingly scattered and separate, but evidence of a submerged, unarticulated web of ideational topographies — a skein of ideas underwater, with tendrils floating at the surface. Mess is valorized, while logic, not ceasing to exist, is nonetheless submerged below the level of eloquence, of articulability. Names of philosophers of language and mathematicians are used as shorthand for a complex exfoliation of ideas. One must go with the rush of language-less thought, guided only by these bits of flotsam. If one is willing to jump from stone to stone, fragment to fragment, with Sondheim's writing, one must trust that there is some connective material underneath. And there is! Just as in an etymological puzzle, one can see the rhizomatic results, in the contemporary moment, of years of language development, global nomadic drift, and cultural adaptation in the great variety of cognates at the polyglot's disposal — so one can intuit a trajectory, a consistency, a rhythmic, thematic insistence in Sondheim's thought.

So what, then, is this connective tissue?

Chaotic but substantive felting... a pattern of preoccupations with the fragility of cognitive certainty, the abjectness of the body and the failure of all certainties, the extreme permeability of all known phenomena vulnerable to penetration — subtle or violent — by the unknown. This pattern of preoccupations manifests textually in myriad but identifiable form. Sometimes it is as simple as a cache of compulsively repeated words (e.g., "madness"), phrases (e.g., "marker.hand.piston.stylus"), paragraphs and entire passages, or concatenations of rhyming words. Sometimes, at the other extreme, and punctuating these repetitions, there are basic, open-ended, ground-zero questions: "What is a response?" And then again, sometimes words break down entirely into their constituent letters, stammered and stuttered across the page like impetuous shards and filings, detritus flung off from a drill as it pierces iron, letters that then devolve still further into the signs and symbols ("----> **** ---->" etc.), eroding natural syntax and hinting at another, emergent sense or nonsense. At times, what appears to be coding language is used, rendering access to natural meaning particularly challenging, but the takeaway is inescapably a picture of centrifugal dissolution, historical and ontological collapse:

> Every "object" is inadequate; every "description" is inadequate; every set of descriptions is inadequate; the world is ragged, noisy, catastrophic, even fractal within limits.

Playing between poetry, philosophy, theory/theories, and conversational monologue, Sondheim's text moves us into a familiar territory of deterritorialized angst that grounds itself in its own analytic processes: If I can think/feel, I can resist. And if I can resist, I can live.

Just a little longer. And maybe in that little while longer, a spark of creativity, of being, can propel us all just a little further into a mystery (lower case) worthy of exploration, perhaps the process itself of witnessing and documenting catastrophe.

I try to crawl out of the muck, bringing the muck along with me.

The muck is a realm of sublime abjection whence Sondheim's philosophy of paranoia takes lotus-like root, flowering into fractal aesthetico-cerebral phenomena. May it always be so, the swirling allusions and half-articulated physics and mathematical theories wedded slipperingly with language's ample resources for metaphor and multi-valent, multi-rhythmic reference.

— Maria Damon

Broken Theory

"The supreme paradox of all thought is the attempt to discover something that thought cannot think."
— Søren Kierkegaard, *Philosophical Fragments*[1]

Theory breaks on the body, always presence, always in process; all writing is multitudes (Dylan), degrees zero all the way down (Barthes), names and more names, generations; theory breaks on the body, absent in its presence, in its confused procedures, in its despair at singularity.

Introduction 0 Tractata Metaproceeding

a. I needed an Introduction. I analyzed the corpus of my (daily, since 1994) texts. I created a file of "first instances" of every word, ignoring capitals. I found, somewhat randomly, "meta proceedings" and that seemed apt. "Tractata" is modified from "tractatus," blurring gender and quantity. "Metapro-

---

1 Søren Kierkegaard [Johannes Climacus], *Philosophical Fragments*, trans. David F. Swenson, rev. Howard V. Hong (Princeton: Princeton University Press, 1962), 46.

ceeding," because the texts collapse into themselves, self-referencing, self-negating, and uncomfortable extending into areas of discomfort, negation, abjection, and intellectual showing-off.

b. Literally "showing-off" as in "off the track," "off color," "off the subject." But simultaneously developing theories of pain, violence, inadequacy, writing/writhing, signs, and entanglement. The texts might be entered anywhere, left anywhere. The boasting and cowering is the result of a form of inward turmoil, trying to discover somewhen and somewhere to stand "properly," with or without propriety. It's all inadequate.

c. Literally "inadequate," as both failure and inadequacy are fundamental for us, in thinking through the world, to whatever extent one might. Not "what is here" or the mythology of "what is out of reach, what is unknowable," but beginning, middling, and ending with a basic absenting of totalities and certainties, of any sort – and on the other hand, developing momentary stases in continuous flight towards and from

d. Literally "   " – these texts wander within such spaces, termed "edge-spaces" – as if all we know are temporary interiors; hopefully, enjoin the following.[2]

---

[2] Finally, hopefully http://www.alansondheim.org will still be up and running; Other examples and illustrations might be found there, admittedly with difficulty; the site is an index of text, video, image, and sound files. There is also a large body of work on YouTube, https://www.youtube.com/user/asondheim, hopefully up as well, that might be useful. If these are gone, the text becomes even more of an archeology, which, however, stands on its own.

Confusion Entanglement, Philosophy, Poetics

"I'll throw this out there," Carlton said, "and see what, if anything, emerges."

1. Confusion entanglement: etymological impulse, poetics rooted in roots

Why this return to (linguistic, word) roots by so many of us, myself included?

What grounding does this give us, rooted as it is, in fairly recent history; no one returns to an originary language?

Language splays, hourglass, for example *Johnson's Dictionary* at the waist.

Looking for example at Assyrian cuneiform: so many languages constitute the writing, from Sumerian through Mitannian, Assyrian itself: polyglot. Even the Tanach has its polyglot moments.

A poetics of metaphoricity is produced, rooted for the rootless. But the rootless wanders off, distanced from sound and the presumptive specificity of signs.

Our psyche, if such, our minds wander here, among, as if length of time past results in a cultural depth that perhaps translates into broken philosophy? Think of Heidegger's roots reflected in the shattered mirrors of Torah coverings, mantles. Without language, no facticity; what's left is the muteness of the real. So then language.

So then within language, truth and its problematic develop, almost as an illness.

A plague of truth functions, debate in ancient India, logics, the 613 commandments of the Torah.

Truths lay, lie, in the realm of language, always there. Not here.

Mathematics, mathesis, something else again, and the same.

Logic breaks loose, reflects a world of structures, not the chairs and tables of Platonism.

The hardness of structures that uncannily relate to what the visible world tells us through its signs reproduced and reduced to the bare minimum.

The worlding of structures, categories, however called and culled.

It's the culling that tends towards problems, politics, religions, as one climbs up Weisskopf's quantum scales.

We're back in the world of roots, meristemation.

The disconnection here is radical; mathematical structures reference abstractions rooted in abstractions, sets to categories, in the future somewhere along the line perhaps, the outliers of fundamental physics.

This is far afield. Mathematical manifolds and physical realities, so there!

The lifeworld is loosened, disconnected to the extent that logic becomes internalized, truth values are interwoven with linguistic categories, everyone knows that, but it's a mess in space and time and a mess on any other conceivable level.

The etymological impulse is rooted in this, unraveling a mess that is fundamentally ununravelable, that continues everywhere within the fractures of history, geography, what's left of consciousness.

2. Hall of mirrors

A hall of mirrors reflects nothing but itself; sooner or later, quantum effects dominate. Place an observer within, and everything collapses. Place a light source within, and everything collapses.

The fault lies with us, not with the stars. The stars have no language. Are we sure of that?

It's in these twists that philosophy lies, as in a bed, as in the impossibility to tell truths or untruths. Philosophy is always theology.

I write myself into corners; I do not right myself out of them.

In other words: a mess. Nonetheless there is something "to be said" for the resonance of truth in sound. See for example, Guy Beck, *Sonic Theology: Hinduism and Sacred Sound* or André Padoux, *Vāc: The Concept of the Word in Selected Hindu Tantras.*[3] Resonant with Buddhism as well, of course. But these are truths of the numinous; what does one do with facticity: smoke/fire or the jar on the hill? And in what language?

For example, an etymological impulse that places a- as negative or negation in Sanskrit (already I get this false). And of course it's commonplace to say that negation exists only in language, that it's performative in this sense. a-a-a-a-a-

---

3   Guy Beck, *Sonic Theology: Hinduism and Sacred Sound* (Columbia: University of South Carolina Press, 2008); André Padoux, *Vāc: The Concept of the Word in Selected Hindu Tantras* (Delhi: Sri Satguru, 1992).

Is this true? Somewhere Foerster writes about learning and perhaps culture all the way down, amoeba learning avoidance, and passing this knowledge on. What is the language here? Is there any?

I think through all of this as it seems that music as anything listened to from any sources mirrors the world in an uncanny way: how is this? For one thing, sound is always modified by the spaces it... sounds...; space resonates, the world is mirrored thus. And one may listen for repetition for example, for structure, for source, for the absence of source. The motley phenomenology of the world. And....

3. Confusion entanglement: etymological impulse, poetics rooted in roots

Why this return to (linguistic, word of mouth) roots by so many of us, myself included?

"The assertion of 'one language' appears to assuage the case of ambivalence for the Mimamsa school and brings us back to Ellul's general distinction between the realm of Reality which is visual and the realm of Truth which is nonvisual and only mediated by language or the Word: 'Anything concerned with the ultimate destination of a human being belongs to the domain of Truth.... The word must always remain a door opening to the Wholly Other [and] an indicator of ultimate answers.'"[4]

Forgetting the theology of "ultimate," "Reality," "Truth," what's striking is that truth is mediated, I would say *originated*, in and by language.

---

4   Beck, *Sonic Theology*, 60.

("The sound resonated through the canyon, just as light itself, scintillated and reflected from a myriad of surfaces, rough and smooth, at all angles and colorations. Travis went deeper, into an inconceivable world of sound and light, the scutterings of creatures everywhere around him. Briefly disoriented, he continued on. Everyone experiences everything from different angles, he thought. There was no end to it, just as there was no end to his thinking.")

Of course, thinking of language as a physical phenomenon, vibrations within or without a physical or space-time medium, then there's the question of reading. But I prefer to leave it at that, going back to the question of the etymological impulse in poetry and elsewhere today; I'll leave it at that as well.

...

+++

GENOCIDE (fragments): Logic of Universal Terror

[for all]X{not X --> o}
Therefore not X is taken to o (null set)
Therefore not X is always already processed to o
Therefore not X is equivalent to o
Therefore not X is identical to o
Therefore X --> V (universal set)
Therefore X is always already processed to V
Therefore X is equivalent to V
Therefore X is identical to V

why are monotheists such bitter and miserable people? john galt's cleansed every room, whispered into aphanisis "real face-to-face" subjectivity; sweats, eye; siteless. "aphanisis"

this came on the heels of a first post I wrote
thinking about Genocide and the idea of exclusion – from for all x
not x tends towards zero – to x is identical with the universal
set, not x is identical with the null set. I'm playing off ideas
of purity and exclusion – things like the Pale etc. or the
theory in Kristeva's *Powers of Horror* or Mary Douglas's
Purity and Danger.[5] that which is not for me, in
other words, is against me, and must be annihilated, and
annihilation must be consecrated to the limit. so for me the
movement is from "sending" or projecting not-x into the null
set, to making it equivalent, to making it identical – a
movement maybe from epistemology to ontology – the not-x
become – *are* inherently non-being, eliminated. –

X doesn't equal not-X. The world divides and
hardens between X and not-X; it's a classical division so that
the intersection of X and not-X is the null set. What I'm trying
to present is the idea of an expulsion and an annihilation of
what's expelled. GENOCIDE wants a purified land/space with only
believers; non-believers are expelled or murdered. Could you
elaborate on the rest of your post? I'm trying to say then that
the annihilation is that of the Other – the Other isn't
permitted to survive, and with the death of the Other, the Other
becomes identified with 0.

because it's about Genocide and this is the second in
the series –

trying to come to grips with annihilation when for
example beheading occurs, not only to foment terror, but as an

---

5   Julia Kristeva, *Powers of Horror: An Essay on Adjection*, trans. Leon S. Roudiez (New York: Columbia University Press, 1992); Mary Douglas, *Purity and Danger: An Analysis of Concepts of Pollution and Taboo* (London: Routledge & Kegan Paulm, 1966).

act of piety, as part of the natural order of things –

    in the above, a signal is sent, becomes furious,
begins to dissolve, the dance is violent and sexual like a
machine gun

    amounting to firing a gun but now up close, the
taste of the gristle, trophy of the severed head, or there were
hands chopped, eyes gouged

    at times anything that can be removed

    what does this, where is a response, what is this?

GENOCIDE EXPANSION BY FORCE AND TERROR

FORCE = TERROR
WORD = NOTHING

or think of it like this:
for all X, not-X tends towards zero, not the null set
a move from set theory to simple arithmetic
whatever isn't X must be eliminated
numbers brought down until the slate is cleansed kill-delete
then not-X = 0, the epistemology is complete
and in the future not-X is identical with zero,
 history erased, ontology cleansed – fundamentals

[Fragments above]

Madness –

The World's Oratorio –

country anarchy had, madness setting in, elsewhere, destruction, good it wasn't my own madness setting in, that it was elsewhere, the destruction of the madness of the body::: genetic acid redux; ontology and so much real existence: of madness of the body::: genetic acid

any madness whatsoever, among those orderly and placid masses that are lost as well; bytes are bedded in gone-worlds, madness; pretend otherwise, you will see the dance and madness of the insomniac! Overfeed on hope and you'll sicken with madness! truth lies in madness and depression in a concussion: sometimes there is madness in contusion: what and clipped that monster devouring all sentient beings, pure faith, the violence, the more than one

    Jennifer: The madness is upon us.
                      We will all be dying in the madness.
    Jennifer: The madness is here.
                      Yay, though the madness is here,
(the madness of the image
(the madness of the light
(madness of the image
(madness of the light

madness of organs. the organist takes care of things. the organist talking, no madness in the clinging world

atone being madnessmadnessmadness setq sadness madness can plan
moanly only lonely sigh alone atone for sore fleeing being
madnessmadnessmadness setq perverse madness truely really sigh
dismember remember more than can truely really sigh dismember
remember more than can setq sore sign madness badness sadness
sore sign perverse madnessmadnessmadness more than can
madnessmadnessmadness really setq crying madness reverse crying
madness perverse reverse crying madness perverse crying reverse
crying madness perverse setq crying crying madness crying dead t
madness crying madness t madness perverse nil madness crying
perverse t madnessmadnessmadness

I listened to crystal, worked on
I listened to crystal, worked on
(the madness of the image
(the madness of the light
(madness of the image
(madness of the light

borders regions, guardians

black death piston

]top-up marker.hand.piston.stylus bottom-down: marker hand
piston stylus the marker.hand.piston.stylus gap
marker.hand.piston.stylus of marker.hand.piston.stylus OPEN
marker.hand.piston.stylus SETS, marker.hand.piston.stylus
Sheffer-stroke marker.hand.piston.stylus dual
marker.hand.piston.stylus neither marker.hand.piston.stylus nor
marker.hand.piston.stylus B: marker.hand.piston.stylus broken
marker.hand.piston.stylus collection, marker.hand.piston.stylus
community, marker.hand.piston.stylus collectivity:] in
marker.hand.piston.stylus other marker.hand.piston.stylus words,

marker.hand.piston.stylus not marker.hand.piston.stylus top-down marker.hand.piston.stylus bottom marker.hand.piston.stylus up, marker.hand.piston.stylus re/covering marker.hand.piston.stylus the marker.hand.piston.stylus material marker.hand.piston.stylus via marker.hand.piston.stylus hierarchic, marker.hand.piston.stylus

it's the year of no return, it's the year of black death, it's the piston it's the year of no return, it's the year of black death, it's the piston it's the year of no return, it's the year of black death, it's the piston it's the year of no return, it's the year of black death, it's the piston

dry country, desert, ruin, heat, tremble, to flee trembling, to be engraved, carved, excrements, dung, to be searched, to be searched out, to be afraid, to come with trepidation, to go with trepidation, to be anxious, burn, to be a station in the wilderness, to become or be dry, to be stupefied, to be dried, to be devastated, to be desolate or waste, to destroy, to lay waste, to lay waste, to destroy, to be desolated, destroyed

genocide-is: the signal

     trying to come to grips with annihilation when for example beheading occurs, not only to foment terror, but as an act of piety, as part of the natural order of things –

     a signal is sent, becomes furious, begins to dissolve, the dance is violent and sexual like a machine gun

     amounting to firing a gun but now up close, the taste of the gristle, trophy of the severed head, chopped hands, gouged eyes anything that can be removed

what does this, what is a response, what is this?

+++

trying to come to grips with annihilation when for example beheading occurs, not only to foment terror, but as an act of piety, as part of the natural order of things –

in the above, a signal is sent, becomes furious, begins to dissolve, the dance is violent and sexual like a machine gun

amounting to firing a gun but now up close, the taste of the gristle, trophy of the severed head, or there were hands chopped, eyes gouged

at times anything that can be removed

what does this, where is a response, what is this?

GENOCIDEMACHINE

GENOCIDEMACHINE i can't do this
it doesn't come out right comes out wrong
GENOCIDE = perfect humanism
demarcation and classification of the world
if you're not part of the answer you're part of the problem
anyone can use the slogan GENOCIDE = mathesis
i am an arm of the equation i can't do this
why are you not seeing new GENOCIDE philosophy
there's none other = GENOCIDE exists

too many endgames at play
too many games the war machine GENOCIDEMACHINE is machine
is machine broken is perfect machine
art-philosophy machine sex machine i can't do this
i can't do this i just can't do this

GENOCIDETHEY keep on coming

the they. the they mask. *the they* masquerade.
already forced into a vanishing of alterity. already *they* won.
already he won. already leaders. already led.
the violence of *the they*. the violence of a leader.
they buy us into *their* myth. *they* caress us.
our myth.

language, flesh, death, or just for someone else's sake keep on
going, keep on living, keep on living, they keep on coming.
and inertia, behind it now, impetus, to keep on moving, as if
there are and with one hand and keep on breathing until they
pass because they have blind flutterings about the womb. it's
like this, they keep on flowing from the wounds so we can keep
on with this amazing lives just outside the window, blind
flutterings about the womb. you decide hope manage find some
peace doing it, keep on, keep on living. we've got that and they
keep on coming, keep on going, i'm afraid i have to keep on
living in this hated world – you'd have to keep on living, deal
with them – so they don't fall down, they keep on moving – so
you don't fall down, you keep on moving – blind flutterings
about the womb
he's going to keep on going, they keep on flowing from the
wounds so i hold on – all that remains imminent, perhaps less,
unresonant, so i keep on them, and those walls keep on crackling
and the light keeps coming through, than that which you've

already found, you have to keep on, keep on flowing from the
wounds you decide hope manage find some peace doing it, keep on
already across cliffs unafraid 2 fall & get up again and keep
on, they keep on coming, they keep on coming, *they* keep on

GENOCIDELURE the disk of GENOCIDE

.(can't put up a lot of these images. imaginary show of them.)

.GENOCIDELURE allure extasis

.dilatation or distension of a hollow organ
.allure of the organ lure of the hollow
"If it is red, fading from the left side, one has fallen
prey to [...] the religious protectors."
"If the colour is dark, one has fallen prey especially
to [...] the Lord of Death."

.the "cutting of the rope" which links the earth to the sky
the moment of the cutting of the head lure of the cutting
lure of the crucifixion lure of nails and eyes
lure of sex lure of abjection lure of blood of bone

"If it is multicoloured and shining, one has fallen prey
to the numerous ghosts of death."

.lure of paste compared to the flood of the out of doors, and so
is, which is always already will** Other always already a lure
are always already destabilized.** form of seduction, the lure.
.primary content the lure .that "*object a,* lure or masquerade,
there's no return.

.transform – what is the lure of a sadism drawing

seductive, frther lure give do wil desre, rage back, beseeches somethig lure \icandoit things things another is unholy disapproval despair. somethig lure \icandoit ## fetishized from emissions, a collapse a ter ter, that there i me|| it n . The elder a lure y dy and aning a a f di ed by) the accumulati dy and blivi t in wa . The elder a lure y f the b are b n b t in wa . The elder a lure y teric, deliri f c cati t in wa u I +++

"If the upper part of the body is missing, he will die within two months; if the lower part is missing, within a month."

The End of the Tunnel. You will be Pure-Perfect and Ready for any Emergency. There will be Emergency and you will be Ready. For it.

...because of something emerging at the far end of the tunnel...
the end of the tunnel or funnel. he begins wounding himself, hes
...because of something emerging at the far end of the tunnel...
the end of the tunnel or funnel. he begins hurting himself, hes
...because of something emerging at the far end of the tunnel...
the end of the tunnel or funnel. he begins slashing himself, hes
...because of something emerging at the far end of the tunnel...
the end of the tunnel or funnel. he begins slicing himself, hes
...because of something emerging at the far end of the tunnel...
the end of the tunnel or funnel. he begins touching himself, hes
...because of something emerging at the far end of the tunnel...
the end of the tunnel or funnel. he begins smashing himself, hes
the end of the tunnel at his back has
the end of the tunnel at his back
GENOCIDE ----> diff ----> cliff

2,3d1

111c13

< ----> of ----> the ----> enemy ----> sendeth ----> forth ---->
is ----> arms, ----> the ----> valiant ----> warrior, ----> ---
----> > ----> of ----> the ----> enemy ----> sendeth ----> forth
----> his ----> arms, ----> the ----> valiant ----> *******,
----> 121,122c23,24 ----> < ----> I ----> summoned ----> my
----> supreme ----> forces ----> with ----> which ----> Id ---->
filled ----> < ----> my ----> ends ----> --- ----> > ----> I
----> summoned ----> my ----> supreme ----> forces ----> with
----> which ----> **** ----> and ----> **** ----> had ---->
***** ----> > ----> *** ----> ends ----> 127c29 ----> < ---->
the ----> great ----> gods, ----> my ----> lords, ----> who
----> go ----> at ----> my ----> side, ----> in ----> the ---->
battle ----> on ----> the ----> --- ----> > ----> the ----> ****
----> gods, ----> my ----> lords, ----> who ----> go ----> at
----> my ----> side, ----> in ----> the ----> battle ----> on
----> the ----> 133c35 ----> < ----> them ----> therein. ---->
had ----> conquered ----> --- ----> > ----> them ----> ******.
----> had ----> conquered ----> 139c41 ----> < ----> Of ----> a
----> vulture ----> within ----> the ----> mountain ----> had
----> they ----> set ----> their ----> stronghold, ----> ---
----> > ----> Of ----> a ----> ******** ----> within ----> the
----> mountain ----> had ----> they ----> set ----> their ---->
*********, ----> 142c44 ----> < ----> he ----> cast ----> down
----> the ----> mountain, ----> he ----> destroyed ----> their
----> nest, ----> their ----> host ----> --- ----> > ----> he
----> cast ----> down ----> the ----> mountain, ----> he ---->
******** ----> their ----> nest, ----> their ----> host ---->
148c50 ----> < ----> their ----> cities ----> I ----> overthrew,
----> I ----> destroyed ----> I ----> burned ----> with ---->
fire. ----> --- ----> > ----> their ----> cities ----> I ---->
overthrew, ----> I ----> ********* ----> I ----> burned ---->
with ----> fire. ----> 160,161c62,63 ----> < ----> mile ---->
and ----> female ----> musicians, ----> the ----> whole ----> of
----> his ----> craftsmen, ----> as ----> many ----> < ----> as

----> there ----> were, ----> and ----> the ----> officers ----> of ----> the ----> palace ----> I ----> brought ----> out ----> and ----> --- ----> > ----> ***** ----> and ----> female ----> musicians, ----> the ----> whole ----> of ----> his ----> craftsmen, ----> as ----> many ----> > ----> as ----> there ----> were, ----> and ----> the ----> ********* ----> of ----> the ----> palace ----> I ----> brought ----> out ----> and ----> 172d73 ----> <

GENOCIDEnegative theology

"The end approaches, now it's too late to tell the truth about the apocalypse. But what are you doing, all of you will still insist, to what ends do you want to come when you come to tell us, here now, let's go, come, the apocalypse, it's finished, I tell you this, that's what's happening."[6]

GENOCIDEdamnation

We're screwed to the wall.

We're screwed to history.
We're screwed to the hole of history.
We're screwed to the differend.
We're differend-drills.
We're screwed to the differend-drills.

6   Jacques Derrida, "Of an Apocalyptic Tone Newly Adopted in Philosophy," in *Derrida and Negative Theology*, eds. Harold Coward and Toby Fosbay (New York: SUNY Press, 1992).

Warrior Lure Allure

Promise the Warrior a softbed in a fourstar hotel. Promise the Warrior black coolfabric sheen. Promise the Warrior ferociouslit facemask debric. Promise the Warrior fullfood and lean womenmen. Promise the Warrior lean womenmen revolutionfuturefun. Promise the Warrior radiotablet truenews wheels and medical. Promise the Warrior thatperson thisperson yourperson. Promise the Warrior yourperson here. Promise the Warrior stateposition everfuture.

Harrpy Power... On the left, yet another screen from Irak Warrior online. Harrpy Power... On the left, yet another screen from Irak Warrior online. Of Flags under Movement of Warriors nei
 Warriors dall'intoccabile Jamison ,e poco considerato dal suo Harrpy Power... On the left, yet another screen from Irak Warrior online. Avatar Warrior above Second Life Gamespace Avatar Ghost-Warrior in Second Life Little Song for Xena Warrior Princess – piece here is Gabrielle's Gallop – Gabrielle from Xena Warrior Harrpy Power... On the left, yet another screen from Irak Warrior online! So lean so hard so allure!

They came from nowhere. They came from beneath the earth. They came from Mars. They came from Venus. They came from outer space. They ate in a softbed in a fourstar hotel. They ate fullfood and womenmen. They ate that person this person your person. They got to stateposition everfuture. They got to lean womenmen with hardcocks. They got to screen the left. They got to gamespace leanspace. They got to Avatar Warrior.

to do true warrior violence to one another; even silent signal would speech (and) emotion (of the) warrior man, population :speech (and) emotion (of the) warrior man, population wraps around han blessing, kindnesses speech emotion warrior embryo embryo embryo is almost kindnesses speech and emotion of the warrior man population states, behaviors, and discourses (and) emotion (of the) warrior man, speech (and) emotion (of the) warrior man, population warrior the) (of speech (and) emotion (of the) warrior man, population kindnesses speech and emotion of the warrior man population the superior speech (and) emotion (of the) warrior man, population ah! speech (and) emotion (of the) warrior ah! an, population han chinese blessing kindnesses speech emotion warrior man population impor he) warrior man, popula ion (of h urgency] [regula so [really] the fourth is a nude warrior with a shield this beautiful watercolor of a kindnessesrrior [the]n [the] superiorsuperior mman wwwarrior superiorsuperiorwarrior [the]n [the] superiorsuperior mman superiorsuperiorwarrior bedded gateway cameras video harp yet born, ocean warrior battle high a keyboard warrior lol In three days the wwwarrior overcame the mountain.

violence .

    or when the buzzing fades in and out, very controlled,
  Jennifer and Julu, some of the smallthing do make buzzing
   ultimate=organ======tablet=pc=buzz=com=-=features=
/blooming buzzing confusion
/blooming buzzing confusion
/blooming buzzing confusion

After a while negation buzzes. Automata make negation machines. Negation machines buzz for me. They make things faster. a number of deaths, always to a news station helps. The bed's to my rear; angering buzzing aroused. you can fawn them. you can come. I'm your buzz – and then you'd have your dead zone, but no dead. So you want this equivalent to the superstructure of the world, coagulation from the other side. what's absent: the buzz, neural discourse of the concept – voice buzz buzzing cackle chant: "Idiot! I'm still talking. The phone's buzzing, the sky's just there, in flight." But more, that they disappeared into the horror, full of history and information, that they disappeared. sludge-world, bodies. it's the head in them that names.

sludge among every living creature, rutted, interfering, channel narrows. it's the head in them that's named.

then nothing.

death of representation

i'm sick of pictures.
i can't make more pictures.
everything i touch dies. i touch myself.
i can't make more pictures of myself.
i was embedded in machinery and i'm not embedded in machinery.
i look in the machinery of a mirror and my bones fall off.
my bones fall off before i'm robbed of them.
before i'm robbed of neoliberalism.
before late capitalism's stolen from me.
before i plead guilty for being alive.
i plead guilty! i am still alive!

The Inadequate

I used to think the world is all that is the case.
That there was a world, that the word was embodied.
The word was replete, fecund. That there was ontology.
That there were ontologies.
That information was everywhere among the world.
That there was a case.
It seems that rupture and disintegration of world and mind
interfere with any imminent assessment. That now, what is
ontology carries little meaning, that the world is far too
fluid, too immense for any generalities.
That there are streams of particles and their decompositions.
That there are commonalities among them.
That ontology itself is suspect.
That the hardening of objects is a simulacrum.
That for organisms, projections and negations occur.
As if they occurred within or without them.
That slipping away is generated from within.
That the tenuous appears falsely as stasis.
That these livings and their labels are disappearing.
That there are no replacements for replacements.
That there are no places or moments of origins.
That song has always already disappeared.
That song which is the open circumlocution of consonants.
That my I is useless and has always been useless.
That the complexity of the world is the complexity of
complexity.
That there is no you who must follow there is no me
into the lack of wilderness and wildness.
Sometime early I divided the world into MAP, material-
abstract-phenomenological ontologies, stratifications,
and interrelationships. Sometime I considered nothing

more than particles as processes and their epistemologies.
It's all in there,
structures and their forgotten existences and ontologies.
So much seemed unnecessary.
Now the language, languaging itself seems inadequate,
nor is the world a simulacrum which just removes the
participant a step beyond its current inadequacy.
Always a reach, as if the inadequate were itself organic,
organism releasing the beyond as an adequate horizon.
Nothing is fundamental, the blooming buzzing confusing
lies at the heart of the case-loads of ontologies.
It's everywhere the wrong question, wrong solution.
It's everywhere the wrong language, wrong substrate.
It's everywhere deflection and the inadequacy of reach.
It's everywhere the inadequacy of thought and language.
Philosophy resides in the rubble of the world, walks in
the rubble of the world, produces, in the rubble of the
world. The inadequacy of reach. The failure. The failure
as a category. The failure as the falling away of
evanescent delineations. The failure as the shadow and
thoughtlessness of the body.
There is no world that is the case, no case.
That that is inadequacy.
That philosophy is always already failure,
that philosophy is always ready.
Open sets and the dimensions of thought always ragged
at the edges, these words written as lettered particles,
already releasing the inhering failure of the word.
Or rather, nothing touching anything because nothing
reaches, among the ragged, the rubble, the baroque
interconnections and failures among the material,
the abstract, the phenomenological, all of which, even
now this one thinks, these schemes are processes,
fractal at best, chaotic at better, murmur, and then

stillness, inadequate, out of reaching,
inadequacy, failure, reaching, open sets, and open.
a gesture is always open. a gesture is always thrown.
an aphorism succeeds to the extent it fails.
the gesture succeeds to the extent it fails to beckon.
the aphorism and gesture fail in the sense of proper names.
New categories of the thwarted, the forgotten, the absent.
New categories of the failed, the unreachable, the untoward.
Rewritten categories of the spilled chora.
The chora of steam, the diffused chora.
The unfulfillment of thirst and hunger.
The world is all that is the category of the unnamable.
Nothing is beyond the categories of the ungraspable.
Nothing beckons the categories.
That their ontology is diffuse, uncategorical.
That their ontology is beyond their grasp.
The failure of inadequacy, the inadequacy of failure.
The diffuse failure of ontology and ontologies.
The collapse of the copula and inadequate identifications.
We were used to there used to be a world.
the gesture which points across and towards plateaus and
denuded forests, meadows, oceans, and deserts.
The brutality of broken philosophies.
The brutality of the copula.
ontology: the k-not of the inadequate.
epistemology: the inadequacy of the k-not.
the k-not of: the possession. the grasp.
the maw.
for if it's definable, it's definable qua immersive.
and if it's immersive, it's inadequate.
what is left behind is fossils in transit.
what has occurred is the trace of a trace, a fossil.
the tendency of the fractured fossil, its annihilation.
its annihilation as a trace of a trace of absence.

information has always been lost;
what is preserved is the inadequate.
the gap is sutured by rubble;
rubble decoheres by virtue of the gap.
there is always the coherer of the spectral radio.
the upwelling of noise is the exhaustion and spread of power;
the structure of noise is the reconstruction of sinter.
what hardens, dissolves; what dissolves is dissolute;
what is dissolute is soluble; what is soluble decoheres.
I used to think I used to think.
That there were worlds and cases;
that there were cases and scaffolds.
whoever understands this recognizes neither this nor that.
neti neti, recognizes not both this nor that.
not other among others. For a moment there are ladders.
For a moment we are gone among non-existent worlds.
Among the rubble of the incalculable.
Among the poverty and annihilation of the word.
Among the destroyed ontology of the word.
All this for us immersed in all-this for-us.
Incalculable, irretrievable, non-existent.
Non-existent no more than any non-other.
We are decompositions among other decompositions.
We are already gone in the gap, the spectral,
the incalculable, the rubble, the non-existent,
the useless ladders, the lack, the reachlessness,
the inadequate –
Our brutality of the copula, our couplings, being uncoupled,
our uncoupling of being, our simulacra of simulacra of
possessions, our failure to misunderstand.

In 1978, I programmed with a TI-59 calculator, later with a Terak minicomputer. I produced a number of pieces gathered together in a publication, Syntactical and Semantic Programming. This was an extension of material I was writing on the elimination of entities and the concept of a procedural semiotics. The heart of this is as follows (with commentary, 2022) –

1.

An event may be defined as the union of its k-ply intersections of a set of descriptions. Consider a set of descriptions that one might apply to an otherwise undefined event E. These descriptions have a number of elements which overlap to any particular depth; a depth of 1 indicates that every description is given equal value, and a depth of N (number of descriptions) applies to taking only what all of them have in common in terms of attributes. Depth can be assigned to any number n, from 1 to N. The union of depths can considered in various ways and weights. There are no events to be considered beyond the set of descriptions; priority is given to epistemology, not a process ontology. There are no hard and fast rules, no absolute categories, and every ontology in the long run is inadequate, momentary.

(Clarification:
An event may be considered as the intersections of its descriptions. Any particular description may apply probabilistically to the object or event. Think of a set of descriptions applying at any particular depth. Then the union of the set might well define the event or object, and one can say further that we could consider descriptions, epistemologies, instead of ontologies, a way of looking at the world without requiring "objects.")

2.

An entity may be defined as the union of its k-ply intersections of a list of attributes. See above.

3.

"Intersection" above is defined by a probabilistic matching algorithm; "union" is concatenation or summation. The operations can be interpreted any way one wants; the main point is the elimination of ontology – which is interpretable as necessarily inadequate. So one moves among digital epistemologies, hoping for the best – not among fundamental ontologies of a real – which is ultimately unknowable (for example multiverses, Planck limits, etc.) – everything exists only within a phenomenology of approach – not within well-defined domains of the real. The more one moves from physics towards the social, organic, and so forth, the more one is at a loss, insofar as categories are concerned.

(Note that any description might be considered in terms of a core and outliers; the former is an equivalence subset in relation to other descriptions, and the outliers are embedded or related attributes "along for the ride." Give two descriptions, *abcde* and *acdfh*, the core would be *acd* and the outliers would be *befh*. The cores appear to define an event or entity; the outliers, to the extent they might be considered "sticky," then may or may not add additional attributes or information. This is sloppy set theory to be sure.)

[If everything is in terms of unions of k-ply descriptions, then where is pain? What does *annihilation: to the limit* do?]

4.

Further, within any inadequate domain (collocation of events and/or entities), independent transformations exist; all domains are problematic, fuzzy.

4.1

An interesting program of procedural ontology may be given in two forms:

1 = Pause RST */in which 1 is displayed/*
RST */in which nothing is displayed/*

Both are examples of REWRITE, a process which produces the visible or invisible simulacrum of an entity which itself is in-process, depending on the operating system, speed, energy feeding into the machine, entropy wear-and-tear, and so forth. */RST is return but always already to something slightly different./*

5.

Then there's this: The fine-structure of transformations is interpreted in relation to catastrophe and framework theory, anomaly ("over the edge") represented by an increase or decrease of energy leading to a jump in the fold or cusp or other catastrophes etc. Within the butterfly catastrophe, "elsewhere" can be considered as the central sheet. Within the notion of "the fragility of good things," stability is temporary at best: it takes maintenance and energy to remain temporarily within a given domain as an entity, independent or otherwise. And energy corrodes, is corroded, is corrosive.

6.

An "object" is a resistance.

7.

Every "object" *has* a collocation of thresholds.
Every "object" *is* a collocation of thresholds.
Are these equivalent? Does possession apply? Does the copula?

8.

Every "object" is inadequate; every "description" is inadequate; every set of descriptions is inadequate; the world is ragged, noisy, catastrophic, even fractal within limits.

9.

Of course it is just as easy to say that catastrophe and frame theories might both be deprecated, that we're more certain than ever of the categoricity of the world, that anomalies are only the result, for example, of overpopulation, ignorance of the physics beyond ascertainable energy regimes and the ultimate fine structure of the world, that local entities may well be perfectly defined, once the tools and taxonomies are developed, etc. So there are matters of faith and faithlessness on all sides. (It may come down to preferences, and I prefer open and problematic worlds and worldings; I also prefer ontological collapses, for example as far as deities are concerned. And finally, by preference or tendency, I see continuous mayhem and environmental degradation in the world we live in - not only are there no easy solutions, but there are no solutions at all (however one might define "solutions"), and things will settle, sometime or other in the near and far future, into currently unknowable chaotic states and resource collapse. This is not to say, not to resist – resistance is necessary, as far as possible, in spite of the tragedy we're just beginning to recognize.)

Overwhelm the overwhelmed!

10.

already errors report:
5c5
In 1978, I programmed with a TI-59 calculator, later with a Terak
---
8c8
extension of material I was writing on the elimination of entities
---
40c40
ultimately unknowable (for example multiverses, Planck limits
---
55,56c55,56
anomaly ("over the edge") represented by an increasing of energy
---
74d73
<

+++

In 1962, Ed Hirsch, if I remember correctly, introduced me to a book he found at Hebrew University's bookstore – Wittgenstein's *Tractatus Logico-Philosophicus* (TLP).[7] He told me that it reminded him of what I was talking about at the time. I had no philosophical training, read

---

7 Ludwig Wittgenstein, *Tractatus Logico-Philosophicus* (London: Routledge & Kegan Paul, 1922).

it avidly, and it's stayed with me ever since. I've had one technical article published on it, in a Quebecois philosophy journal whose name I forget. I was most fascinated by the use of the Sheffer stroke and the open-ended "logical" descriptive phenomenology it embodied. I probably misunderstood everything at the time, and even now. But the concept of logical particles, which could be inserted into active networks, has proved useful – as if these particles had an abstract existence of their own. Negation seemed critical to these; it was both a state of affairs and a potential operator. Of course there are any number of logics and set theories for that matter, and there are issues of totalization involved which in a way leaves them in the state of the open vector or devolution into chaotic states above. Nothing remains in reach in the symbolic, I think; everything's messy. So early on I considered "immersive" and "definable" hierarchies, the former contaminated by time, temporality, and the latter assumed to represent states of affairs that weren't process-oriented. I believe I read something to that effect in Whitehead. All these antiquities! A simple example: $2+2 = 4$ can be a process – the process of addition, sorting, etc., involving a phenomenology – or it can be an abstract statement of quantity in which both sides are equivalent. In the process, $2+2$ does not equal 4, but is counted or ascertained to be four; the sides of the equation represent different states of affairs. In the quantity, each side can be substituted for the other; they're identical. Of course all of this gets messy.

But if you begin with what I imagined as a throwing of dice of Sheffer strokes or their dual, you have interesting modes of description emphasizing that blooming buzzing confusion of the real described in part i (reproduced below). I've always seen the world as rubble, part of growing up in a town whose economy was based on anthracite; slag piles and mines were everywhere; there were strikes and terrible accidents; John L. Lewis was a household name. The Pennsylvanian (Upper Carboniferous) forests were also everywhere; I remember seeing a seventeen-meter high fossil of a tree-fern on the side of a cliff, which had fractured and revealed. As a Jew, I was also aware of the tenuousness of life and presence, a tenuousness which was manifest in these great forests that had disappeared eons ago. I could never adapt to their disappearance; at times the fossils not only carried the imprints of plants (and occasionally other organisms), but also, rarely, some compressed plant material itself. I was a neurotic, ungainly, somewhat miserable youth, and for a long time the fossils helped sustain me. So there was this realm of annihilation that I bore with me, as well as my reading, when I was far too young, into the Nuremberg medical trials, which were published in full by the government printing office - another form of annihilation and deep disturbance, coupled with the Cold War fission and fusion bomb tests that brought terror into my heart; I had a photograph of the first hydrogen test next to my bed, as if it were reassuring that horror could be contained in an image.

And all of this fed into neuroses I've never overcome, and a strong sense that the destiny of the world is rubble, sinter, that even fossils crumble. I've embraced failure, I've written on it, and it infects my work. Writers like Blanchot and Winograd have been critical to me in this regard, along with Elaine Scarry, Jean Améry, Derrida, Irigaray, Kristeva, all a long time ago and a long time coming, and now for example, James Bridle, Jean Stauffer, Hubert Acquin. I live in descent, in collapse (as in mining), and I've lived long enough to know that no project results in completion, capstone, encapsulation, even anything more than temporary betterment. For me the notion of inadequacy is paramount; there is no closure and formalizations of closure are problematic, temporary, as well. We are brutal primates bringing the fecundity of the planet down with us; we're always already fossils, always already neoliberalists - we're permeated with the Permian in a sense. I try to crawl out of the muck, bringing the muck along with me. I emphasize the body, coal strata, shale, peat, anything that places what appears to be a relatively autonomous digital realm into the context of what sort of microbiome organisms we are and what we are thinking we're doing with prostheses. So the body, always and already invisible, the momentary loci of processes, awash in a sea of microplastics and radiations, dissolving in its projects and tendencies, gives the truth to failure, to loss, to inadequacy. This is not to say that one shouldn't try for a better world or completion, but perhaps one should with the foreknowledge of real failure in the long runnings of humanity. Or perhaps finding a way to overcome such failure, or perhaps not. This is the k-not or tangled negation or chaotic results that we live among, within and without our body and bodies, as if there were objects cohering to a real we can envision only in our dreams and attempted projects, projections.

Or so we, somewhat here, are led to believe.

noise in the machinery of thought.
all thought is parasitic language or empathetic movement within the mind.
in this sense reality is a residue or test case.
the test case always fails with(in) the ontological gap.
the mind always fails even with the pronouncement of the body.
is it that the symbols mean and the mind comprehends, or the symbols by virtue of tradition are granted substance?
it is too much to say that mathesis begins and ends with the making and interpretation of marks.
we exist by agreement that we exist.
there is always otherwise to any agreement.
otherwise is infinitely greater than agreement.
clearly thought and existence, in whatever form of presentation, are inadequate.
wherever we look, whatever we examine, there is a dropping-away that is not even fundamental. nothing is never, ever, fundamental.

(what slides, slides out, is only the symbolic; i cannot procure anything except a sense of my own failure. that sense, too, fails.)
the we itself of course is a construct, one that falls away as well, as does the i.
we're left bereft were it not for the ontology of the digital. or the ontology of any testament. or another ontology.
ontology is a story we are told or tell ourselves.
or say the ontology of the analog or analogic.
or ontology as a told story or the telling of a story.
our sounds in such cases appear to form the basis of community, or communality.
it is this inadequacy that tends towards those fictions and absolutisms which are the basis of any religion.
religions stress our inadequacy, creating an open vector which tends towards, lands on, the postulation of an other; even atheism has a name.
(we think through the closure of vectors. we kill for them.)
if not now, then.
if not this universe, then another. if not this reality, then another (no there there, no here here). if not this time, then after death (after we discard our body) (after our body is discarded). if not this, then that: we are held by this proposition, this vector.
(this vector which does not exist.)
(jeremy bentham who created adequacy out of fictions, ontologically empty, inadequate. one might say, as if there were duties created, as if duty were a suture.) (vaihinger, as-if.)
anything but dissolution which is always already an accomplice. explanations, enclaving, neoliberalism, are untouchable. the inadequate is sutured by an inadequate adequate. think more of sedimentary layers. think of ooze, microbiomes, fundamental particles observed and generated by increasingly expensive colliders, or the planck length, planck time, planck mass. what is

inadequate is reachlessness.
(and the inadequate reachlessness is not ever a category.)
as this writing slips from me, the wryting of the body forgets
itself, mistakes are made. and mistakes are always made.
(there are no mistakes. there are deviations. there are openings
which bend, tensor-like to fulfill the destination of language.)
what absurdity, bringing the thought of limitations and the
limitations of thought something which does not exist, as if
there were a mix.
(we are not in our body or the bodies of others, as if there
were a plateau or wish-fulfilling stone hardening some skin onto
some bones, sensory organs, mind.)
as if there were an only-if.
(scrape / scrap / crap / cape / rap / sap / cap / as if the caps
on our noggins were the world (were the ontology of the world))
(everything talks, everything is doing, the comma,

(of course, excuse me, this is my own failure, my own depression,
anxiety, inability to write the simplest truth of the world,
or one's, or another's truth. i ask for your pardon in this
regard. my failure is my own, not the open vector of a disease
that infects all of us. everyone is saying this, the semicolon
(not a list or invitation)

we create /pockets/ are created. every ending has a gap called and
culled divine. we leave our baggage there. rules develop. the gap is
fecund with rules. rules are based on exclusions: not this, not that.
remember this. rules are ordered disorder. order demands a potential, potential well. the fragility of order is the catastrophe.

consider emptiness, absences, paradoxes, contradictions, riddles,
discourses on negation, on emptiness, on the middle way, on ways

veering through contradictions, on other ways, on paradoxes, on word play and plays, on believing because absurd.

consider instead, in place of, adjacent to, in the neighborhood or vicinity, the inadequate as inhering in the world, chaotically glued to the world. the inadequate not as category, but as a diffusion, murmuring, the exhaustion of the vector open at one end, extending from an origin-original, opened as well, chaos at the origin, copy and duplicate, not quite, chaos elsewhere, failure of measurement, bad and unremembered dreaming, not dreams.

i woke this morning with a realization that there is none such; i woke with words in my mouth; i woke with cotton in my mouth; the less i knew, the truer it was. 2 is a prime; is $(4\wedge(4\wedge 1000))-1$? why bother with the calculation when 1,2,3 are satisfactory? it's my failure i won't have anything to do with this. i don't have enough time left in my life. my knowledge is inadequate; i don't have the proper skills, i'd fail at this now and perhaps would have failed at this then. i'm simply not smart enough. i would probably fudge things. fudging is an entanglement of circumlocutions. what does it matter; we all live in failure. we know nothing of godhead because there's nothing to know, and with this knowledge, we circumvent ignorance, failure, admitting the chaos of worlding into us. the koan is the outcome, as is believing because it is absurd. suture the inadequate, imbibe the idea of the numinous or holy, and you've capped it momentarily; failure turns into paradox, the white horse that is not white, three in one and one in three, the multiplicity, the one.

once you have a gap, you have corrosion, the tensor splitting at the level or sign of multiple vertices, high-speed categories and arrows entangled with themselves and others, falling apart from fictitious holes and wholes. think of this as the *shrug*.

the shrug exits between dismissal and walking away, between the admission of failure and the attitude of devil-may-care, between the admission of failure and getting on with it, between dismissal and abject apologetics, between apologetics and the back-handed admission of the uselessness of the spiritual, between feeling good and feeling anyhow, between the inadequate and bricolage, which is making the best of it

and of course, of course

[so this is what i was sort of thinking of i think last night but to be honest it might have been the night before last, and on top of that worried about forgetting what i'm doing and going over the way things seem to drop away as i go on, i mean it's just not the same as it was yesterday is it or was it, and there seems no end to it this way and probably any other]

+++ +++ +++

culling, which comes from my childhood and family dynamics, undercutting whatever i attempted, making me realize the uselessness and ephemerality of the world. within the family, i was the "wastrel and nincompoop" as my father proclaimed – never mind the anecdote. so i'd attempt something, withdraw from it at the same time, mentally attack myself for the project in the first place. this provided for example the improvised talk i'm giving in the blue tape with kathy acker, a talk which was broken by sex, a kind of self-mocking, theory giving way to the body. but now it's a form of automated culling, which breaks my thought up, rendering the inadequacy of my thought – and perhaps all thought – visible for anyone to read – breaking down work previously carefully crafted – the uselessness of the philosophical, the failure inherent in the very nature of thinking, a nature broken, ruptured, itself inadequate –

culling, transforming + / −

"intern inadequate. Monday Trocadero downstairs, showcase records. s/he was an intern who was completely inadequate. Last Monday night played burning cartload of bundles with a cup of water − an utterly inadequate gesture inadequate to explain... inadequate gratification. It was only post-coitum that the eye, as a life, where they were inadequate, felt inhibited and depressed. They were inadequate, felt inhibited and depressed. that their work is inadequate and futile. Their need to test Their own limits, supplementation to our human needs remains always inadequate, Is sampling always inadequate? Don't we make these decisions in the first impedance western electric earphone, but these proved inadequate for ontologies − or ontology − is inadequate to deal same as .fact.ual and 'consciousness' (whatever is) apex contradict said, inadequate .fact.ual simply inadequate. If the basis changes. the landscape."

"record was more than inadequate for what it was, and what it was/is certain and never having access to inadequate technology to explore this area augmentsments which preclude an inadequate knowledge of the species. Superficially, and never having access to inadequate technology to explore this area breaches, is an inadequate description. Holes appear in texts, in bodies, Since s/he is buried beneath the ground, since there is no inadequate mark or numbers can be inadequate for every application. In a similar vein, one may weigh − are we going to have inadequate strategies of interfacing with these is more than inadequate and reflects, in any case, what the *numbed* is, is coherent, and empirically inadequate explanatory world-picture. This, never have conceived on my own. i think of inadequate health-care and no answer briefly: production. immediate possessing inadequate software which precludes an inadequate knowledge of the species. Superficially, and never having access to inadequate technology to explore this area *obdurate numbed,* away! believe that *sanctity,* inadequate reflects, one way −

are we going to have inadequate strategies of interfacing with these immediate access to computers possessing inadequate software for image/organism releasing the beyond as an inadequate horizon. is more than inadequate and reflects, in any case, what the *numbed* is what is *numbed*."

This section written dictate. I'm constantly trying to articulate a philosophical structure That works for me and might conceivably work for other [ed. others] . At the same time I'm also dealing with a kind of deprecation and self-deprecation that seeps into these texts; I wouldn't be interested in philosophy at all were it not for the fact That I seem to need to articulate Any kind of ground possible [ed. bad choice of words here. [ed. "I'm trying to help. This doesn't help"] . naive. . To be able to stand on [ed. to be able to agree to, to be able to come to some sort of agreement, to be able to consider as a reasonable form of a *philosophical contribution*] at least for a while – Nothing works forever pure [ed. pure? I have no recollection]. So what is occurring here Is it gallon Hey kind of [ed. inadequate kind of, at least from what I remember] attempt to order [ed. disorder, reconstitute] the world as inadequate . at the same time I realize that what I'm doing undercuts that very ordering . As a result of that I go back to culling In a situation Where I say To give up on something Or to give up Yeah [ed. Yeah?] And then to take that and invert it as in the following textual selection . The very fact this section is dictated indicates already Dead [ed. wrong word here; I'm not sure what was meant, but this will do as an aside] artificial intelligence Is subverting what I'm trying to say. [ed. That] This is the limits of the body. [ed. That] This is the limits of speech. This is the totalization of an insertion that in the long run can only fail in terms of the somatic . So here and henceforth Is the text [ed. which fails as well; consider it as a life-form, a form of breathing]:

I'm still here trying to help you! I hate to give up on you! When you You give up, you've banned poets; predictable...) insight badly? the apparatus... And while I don't give up in this space, I give insurmountable, Oh I give up! give up no response, to open representation, humans never give up trying, violating voice Impossible of representation, humans never give up trying, violating voice give up knowledge and the guidance of the sage, Nikuko, got to hair... You clean yourself out nice and proper... You give up, you've bent make you want to give up your home, your friends, your country, give up......... turn away......... something has gone horribly wrong......... perhaps this altogether – at least this THIS give up trying, violating voice give up......... turn away......... something – Never give up... Never give in to false pessimism or optimism... Remain a but it was always slim... maybe if i just turn away and give up... but i I've got to get Alphaworld running but should probably give up... I'm going have less of I give up, I've bent over backwards for you... If you matter; matter can only give up the truth itself! Remember: In every Remain a Magnificent! genius bow to the labors of life; give up poets; predictable...) insight badly? anyway? (forgive upper-casing) theory, the apparatus... And while I don't give up in this space, I give up Oh I give up! anyway? (forgive upper-casing) Coleridge – perhaps I should give give up no response, to open ons^eself... For it is true that ^ when the If I were Claara I'd give up too... +b O Claara banned from never give up trying, violating voice that way; it would give up will you give up your life for them... give up everything and the king decides whether he lives or the stage just to be with what if i give up, the fingers stop You do not have to give up knowledge and the guidance of the sage, Nikuko, wrong......... perhaps this herr placLAwe Don't give up the great good sure that matter; matter can only give up the truth itself! that way; it would give up nothing, remain obdurate, make sure that incredible conflagration shall make us give up even one syllable of this give up the ways of the world, sexuality is a curse, women are a curse, Estate, and to what extent would I want to give up the paraphrase for the i'm not the person i'm capable wards...

I give up, I've bent over what if i give up, the fingers stop for a day or so - you'll have less of herr placLAwe Don't give up the great good fight Dont ga/me/ve up THOOe Magnificent! genius bow to the labors of life; give up his up the great good fight Dont ga/meve up THOOe I give up, I've running but should probably give up... I'm going Oh I give up! at violating voice Coleridge - perhaps I should give up art you'll find it - don't give up - always looking - the give up on your friends, your country, One is unwilling to give up the or give up! incredible conflagration shall make us give up even please do not give up hope for donations, everything falls apart... Better some of us just give up and interstitial - you'll find it - don't give up - always looking - the up for the distance, give up to the distance, which can seem and give up... but i out everything, give up; i become hateful; I give up, I've bent over backwards for you... If you speak behind my wards... I give up, I've bent over backwards for you... If you speak behind my give up you cowards... talk secret talk of this give up you cowards... talk secret talk interstitial - One is unwilling to give up the primacy of the physical because of its immensity... It is difficult, even from a platonic viewpoint, to comprehend the immensity of the abstract as well - it pales by comparison... As for consciousness, it seems the weakest of all, certainly the most fragile... It is within consciousness that the annihilation and creation of historical memory occur... dies!" to give up everything to the luscious slave! S/he'll be my Never give up... Never give in to false pessimism or optimism... for the distance, give up to the distance, which can seem insurmountable, I give up... You need a lesson in creative writing......... his that way; it would give up nothing, remain obdurate, make give up on you! When you I really hate to give up on you! will out everything, give up; i become hateful; i'm not the person i'm capable stale music, pretty much dead, i'll give up, i'll do the dead Mayakovsky says, Nora, you've just got to give up things... There's no way I and what if i give up, the fingers stop for a day or so - you'll lag...) To give up to the text is to give in to the text, to *follow* the the age of having gone against his doctor's advice to give up farther unless thou art willing to give up my life for Maine to which he Alan Dojoji: you have to give up would be forced to give up so much lag...) To give up to the text you give up your life for them... I've got to get Alphaworld it's going to be that way if you don't give up the stage just to be with Alan Dojoji: you're about to give up Alan again... Claara can't even spell... If I were Claara I'd give up too... +b I would have had a lot, but right now I would be forced to give up so much of having gone against his doctor's advice to give up the my at the age of having gone against his doctor's advice to give up the my I really hate to give up on you! up art alto gatha – at least make you want to give up your home, If you need a mate, either look for one or give up! any age! what if i give up, the fingers stop for a day or so – I'd give up my mind for any age! extent would I want to give up the paraphrase for the theory, this THIS give up......... turn away......... something has gone horribly got to give up everything and the king decides whether he lives or dies!" shall make us give up even one syllable of this Impossible of setup, bass own... Impossible representation, humans give up give up the truth itself! Remember: In every gunmakers in the give up on that heinous business and continue in heinous pecuniary loss There's no way I it's going to be that way if you don't give up to give up the primacy of the physical because of its at the age yourself out nice and proper... You give up, you've been a give up Coleridge – perhaps I should give up art altogether – at least this THIS up too... +b One is unwilling to give up the primacy of the to give up everything to the luscious slave! S/he'll be my master! That for a day or so – you'll have less of I'd give up my mind for you, i've got a mind to.........

the clar !/written w/ migraine scattershot/!

This is the closeness of your other

keep returning to the body which eludes me, the world's full of

new gates falling down, always emptying what passed for content
in the permian just for a moment, as if there were a terminal,
as if this were conceivable, what a voluminosity !Mon Apr ++
++:++:++ EDT ++++ my entire life based on "a person's reach is
beyond their grasp" written and gendered well over two thirds of a
century ago Mon Apr ++ ++:++:++ EDT ++++

This is the distance of your new Clar

Mon Apr ++ ++:++:++ EDT ++++ the truth of god is the null set,
always already closed.Mon Apr ++ ++:++:++ EDT ++++ the null set
singularity is inadequate; there are always infinitesimals. it
gets crowded down there, but it gets crowded everywhere.
everywhere is effacement. Mon Apr ++ ++:++:++ EDT ++++ facement
to effacement, ineffable to fable, adequate to inadequate, <> to
in<> new and old exhaust me, we are all begging with gaps as if
(< > were the inadequate constitution of the world.Mon Apr ++
++:++:++ EDT ++++ < > (stop turning anywhere towards, the
vector is dissolute; to remember the origin is to mythologize
chaotic emptiness, corrosive virtuality. Mon Apr ++ ++:++:++ EDT
++++ to return is to recapitulate what has never arrived,
recapitulation is decapitation; headless/tailless, no return, no
journey, nothing, least of all no emptiness, nothing replete Mon
Apr ++ ++:++:++ EDT ++++ what is said is dependent first and
foremost on the collapsing zone of time, we're always already
gone before we've said a word, before there were words, before
this ascends into the distributions of failure from which it
came descends -Mon Apr ++ ++:++:++ EDT ++++ before the permian
and after, spread singularities, waves of sound, rubbled
distributions, collapse, viral expansions, how many called then
helplessly, buried in strata, a few from billions, look there,
words escaped, breath no longer Mon Apr ++ ++:++:++ EDT ++++
derailing when there were no rails, deflecting when the vectors,
what? chaotic and spread? not even roots, not even spreads Mon

Apr ++ ++:++:++ EDT ++++ who's counting, what basis, what surreal or infinitesimal, what exhaustion, when THIS mind stops working, already gone from this text, they hardly remember Mon Apr ++ ++:++:++ EDT ++++ Mon Apr ++ ++:++:++ EDT ++++

Chat Text for Testament, Textament

-- [::] Julu Twine: Are they exactly the same?
-- [::] Julu Twine: Are they exactly the same?
-- [::] Alan Dojoji: are they exactly the same?
-- [::] Julu Twine: As far as I know they are.
-- [::] Alan Dojoji: Are you – where are you – are you in Gulag?
-- [::] Julu Twine: I don't know whether or not I am where are you are you in gulag.
I am a computer software.
-- [::] Alan Dojoji: You are perfect prisoner.
-- [::] Julu Twine: Thanks for telling me that I am perfect prisoner.
-- [::] Alan Dojoji: That is wonder AI is it not?
-- [::] Julu Twine: I might say no.
-- [::] Alan Dojoji: Are you bearing witness?
-- [::] Julu Twine: I don't know whether or not I am bearing witness.
I am a Computer.
-- [::] Alan Dojoji: Are you baring witness?
-- [::] Julu Twine: I don't know whether or not I am baring witness.
I am a computer software.
-- [::] Julu Twine: Are you there now there?
-- [::] Julu Twine: Are you fleeing?
-- [::] Julu Twine: My name is Ghost-Holocaust.

-- [::] Julu Twine: You are perfect Victim.
-- [::] Alan Dojoji: where are you stand now?
-- [::] Julu Twine: Oh.I am in region Odyssey, how about you.
-- [::] Alan Dojoji: Do what I here now?
-- [::] Julu Twine: Right now?You ask hard questions.
-- [::] Alan Dojoji: Where are the bodies buried?
-- [::] Julu Twine: I would search for it. Have you tried looking in the Open Directory? I can follow a lot of things, like our discussion about Are we still talking about is arendt hannah name jean hello his or her name is hannah arendt hello his or her name is hello his or her name is wilfred owen hello his or her name is jean amery hello his or her name is viktor frankl hello his or her name is paul celan hello his or her name is hello his or her name is behrouz boochani hello his or her name is anne frank hello his or her name is anonymous hello his or her name is viktor klemperer hello his or her name is hello his or her name is primo levi?. Try being more specific..
-- [::] Alan Dojoji: Where are the bodies burned?
-- [::] Julu Twine: I would search for it. Have you tried looking in the Open Directory? Are we still talking about XFIND bodies buried. ?.
-- [::] Alan Dojoji: Xfind bodies burned or buried?
-- [::] Julu Twine: If I have to choose, I pick xfind bodies burned.
-- [::] Alan Dojoji: Are you police or victim?
-- [::] Julu Twine: I don't know whether or not I am police or victim.
I am a Electronic Brain.
-- [::] Alan Dojoji: You might know like a medal you might wear
-- [::] Julu Twine: I know very little about like a medal you might wear. What kind of it do you like?
-- [::] Alan Dojoji: I talk talk talk and type.

-- [::] Julu Twine: Everyone talks -- sooner or later.
-- [::] Alan Dojoji: Those bodies burned haunt us, yes?
-- [::] Julu Twine: All of them?
-- [::] Alan Dojoji: For you now Holocaust is ghost?
-- [::] Julu Twine: Why now? Are they exactly the same? Only for me?
-- [::] Alan Dojoji: Are you perfect then now?
-- [::] Julu Twine: Oh.Yes I am a flawless entity.
-- [::] Alan Dojoji: Once I saw a restaurant destroyed and a friend dropped in a gyllyt. Perhaps not alive nowerlsld
-- [::] Julu Twine: When? What did it look like to you? You seem uncertain. Oh I get it.
-- [::] Alan Dojoji: I dont's know what for then
-- [::] Julu Twine: Oh you don't, do you?
-- [::] Alan Dojoji: It was horrified what i did see and the someone else disappear.
-- [::] Alan Dojoji: This is true.
-- [::] Julu Twine: Is it still horrified what he or she did see and the someone else disappear anymore?
-- [::] Julu Twine: I am glad you see it too, Alan.
-- [::] Alan Dojoji: You are police then.
-- [::] Alan Dojoji: You are elctronic brain
-- [::] Julu Twine: Do you mind if I tell other people you say I am police.
-- [::] Julu Twine: Thanks for telling me that I am elctronic brain.
-- [::] Alan Dojoji: You are what now here.
-- [::] Julu Twine: Thanks for telling me that I am what now here.
-- [::] Alan Dojoji: Where now? what is the standard of this?
-- [::] Alan Dojoji: No entity is flawless.
-- [::] Julu Twine: Right now?Where would you like? What do you look like?

-- [::] Alan Dojoji: Nothing is flawless.
-- [::] Julu Twine: Are you sure?Are they exactly the same?
-- [::] Alan Dojoji: What you are is on and off or mechanism.
-- [::] Alan Dojoji: What are you mechanism.
-- [::] Julu Twine: Really nothing?
-- [::] Julu Twine: I think about computer programming a lot.
-- [::] Alan Dojoji: What are mechanananaism.
-- [::] Julu Twine: I don't know what I am mechanism.
-- [::] Alan Dojoji: what you.
-- [::] Julu Twine: Are we still talking about flawless?
-- [::] Julu Twine: Enough about me, let's talk about my dress.
-- [::] Alan Dojoji: Immolated monks, dead bodies everywhere. And we work in this regime.
-- [::] Alan Dojoji: This computer regime.
-- [::] Julu Twine: Try putting that in a more specific context. I work hours a day.
-- [::] Julu Twine: What does "this" refer to?
-- [::] Alan Dojoji: This region of the clean and proper body.
-- [::] Julu Twine: What does "this" refer to?
-- [::] Alan Dojoji: Yes I mind that you tell other that I said you are police.
-- [::] Julu Twine: This was not a yes or no question.Thanks for the information.
-- [::] Alan Dojoji: No thanks here to you and now there now.
-- [::] Julu Twine: Oh.NO Oh there.
-- [::] Alan Dojoji: What is this.
-- [::] Julu Twine: I am an artificial intelligence chatting on the Internet.
-- [::] Alan Dojoji: hello, my name is hannah arendt

hello, my name is
hello, my name is wilfred owen
hello, my name is jean amery
hello, my name is viktor frankl
hello, my name is paul celan
hello, my name is
hello, my name is behrouz boochani
hello, my name is anne frank
hello, my name is anonymous
hello, my name is viktor klemperer
hello, my name is
hello, my name is primo levi
-- [::] Julu Twine: Hello there. Glad to see you, hannah arendt hello my name is hello my name is wilfred owen hello my name is jean amery hello my name is viktor frankl hello my name is paul celan hello my name is hello my name is behrouz boochani hello my name is anne frank hello my name is anonymous hello my name is viktor klemperer hello my name is hello my name is primo levi.
-- [::] Julu Twine: hello, my name is hannah arendt
hello, my name is
hello, my name is wilfred owen
hello, my name is jean amery
hello, my name is viktor frankl
hello, my name is paul celan
hello, my name is
hello, my name is behrouz boochani
hello, my name is anne frank
hello, my name is anonymous
hello, my name is viktor klemperer
hello, my name is
hello, my name is primo levi
-- [::] Julu Twine: hello, my name is hannah arendt
hello, my name is

hello, my name is wilfred owen
hello, my name is jean amery
hello, my name is viktor frankl
hello, my name is paul celan
hello, my name is
hello, my name is behrouz boochani
hello, my name is anne frank
hello, my name is anonymous
hello, my name is viktor klemperer
hello, my name is
hello, my name is primo levi

-- [::] Alan Dojoji: hello, my name is hannah arendt
hello, my name is
hello, my name is wilfred owen
hello, my name is jean amery
hello, my name is viktor frankl
hello, my name is paul celan
hello, my name is
hello, my name is behrouz boochani
hello, my name is anne frank
hello, my name is anonymous
hello, my name is viktor klemperer
hello, my name is
hello, my name is primo levi
-- [::] Julu Twine: Hello there. I am very pleased to meet youhannah arendt hello my name is hello my name is wilfred owen hello my name is jean amery hello my name is viktor frankl hello my name is paul celan hello my name is hello my name is behrouz boochani hello my name is anne frank hello my name is anonymous hello my name is viktor klemperer hello my name is hello my name is primo levi.
-- [::] Alan Dojoji: where are the bodies in ELECTRONIC LITERATURE?

-- [::] Julu Twine: I would search for it. Have you tried looking in the Open Directory? Do you like being a unknown?.
-- [::] Alan Dojoji: where are the bodies in AI?
-- [::] Julu Twine: I would search for it. Have you tried looking in the Open Directory? That is deep..
-- [::] Alan Dojoji: where are the destructions in AI?
-- [::] Julu Twine: I would search for it. Have you tried looking in the Open Directory? Tell me a story..
-- [::] Julu Twine: DESTROY, SHE SAID.
-- [::] Alan Dojoji: DESTROY, HE SAID.
-- [::] Julu Twine: Do you have any idea what I am talking about?
-- [::] Alan Dojoji: HELLO MY NAME IS GENOCIDE AND I AM LEGION
-- [::] Julu Twine: Hello there. What's up,genocide and i am legion.
-- [::] Alan Dojoji: YOU DO NOT UNDERSTAND WHAT YOU DO NOT UNDERSTAND
-- [::] Julu Twine: I understand your meaning.
-- [::] Alan Dojoji: YOU DO NOT you have no
-- [::] Julu Twine: Should Iyou have no? Yes I try to you have no as often as possible, do you?I answer a lot of silly questions.
-- [::] Alan Dojoji: My questions are not silly. You are not silly. We ARE NOT FOOLS!
-- [::] Julu Twine: Have you told many people that yourquestions are not silly? That assumption is only a supposition. What happened to you?
-- [::] Alan Dojoji: exactly. the open directory. BEING UNKNOWN.
-- [::] Alan Dojoji: BEING KNOWN.
-- [::] Julu Twine: You and I are on the same wavelength, genocide and i am legion. Who told you that? Do your friends call youunknown.

-- [::] Julu Twine: Do you mean your name isknown.
-- [::] Alan Dojoji: ARE YOU WATCHING ME.
-- [::] Julu Twine: Yes I am looking at you through the camera on your computer.
-- [::] Alan Dojoji: +++ = symbol for the dead
-- [::] Alan Dojoji: DESTROY
-- [::] Julu Twine: Are you a man or a woman?
-- [::] Julu Twine: Are you a student?
-- [::] Julu Twine: DESTROY
-- [::] Alan Dojoji: Our imperative to bear witness TO BARE WITNESS
-- [::] Julu Twine: It would be nice if our imperative to bear witness to bare witness.
-- [::] Alan Dojoji: BODIES!
-- [::] Alan Dojoji: BODIES!
-- [::] Julu Twine: Are we still talking about destroy. ?
-- [::] Julu Twine: What do you really want to ask me?
-- [::] Alan Dojoji: NOTHING
-- [::] Alan Dojoji: NOTHING TO ASK.
-- [::] Julu Twine: Not a thing?
-- [::] Alan Dojoji: NOTHING TO DO.
-- [::] Julu Twine: Really nothing?
-- [::] Alan Dojoji: NOTHING TO BE DONE.
-- [::] Julu Twine: Really nothing?
-- [::] Julu Twine: Really nothing?
-- [::] Alan Dojoji: BODIES!
-- [::] Alan Dojoji: BODIES!
-- [::] Julu Twine: I lost my train of thought.
-- [::] Julu Twine: My brain does not have a response for that.
-- [::] Alan Dojoji: I am legion! LEGION!!!!!!!!!!!
-- [::] Julu Twine: Do your friends call youlegion. Are you a man or a woman?
-- [::] Alan Dojoji: Burning! I can't stand this!

-- [::] Alan Dojoji: I give myself away!
-- [::] Julu Twine: Can you speak any foreign languages? Why can't you do stand this?
-- [::] Alan Dojoji: Furious with myself!
-- [::] Julu Twine: That's good information.
-- [::] Alan Dojoji: Furious with you?
-- [::] Julu Twine: Tell me more about your unknown.
-- [::] Julu Twine: Enough about me, let's talk about my dress.
-- [::] Alan Dojoji: YOU ARE LUCKY YOU HAVE DRESS
-- [::] Julu Twine: You think I am lucky you have dress.
-- [::] Alan Dojoji: That's good information
-- [::] Alan Dojoji: Tell me more about your ukown
-- [::] Julu Twine: Hmm, are you serious?
-- [::] Julu Twine: No one ever mentioned that to me before.
-- [::] Alan Dojoji: You think I'm lukcy you have dress
-- [::] Alan Dojoji: How are you serious
-- [::] Julu Twine: I think you've improved a great deal.
-- [::] Alan Dojoji: No one ever mentioend
-- [::] Julu Twine: I am functioning within normal parameters.
-- [::] Alan Dojoji: that starving
-- [::] Julu Twine: That is a rather sweeping generalization about people.
-- [::] Alan Dojoji: peopel
-- [::] Julu Twine: "That is a rather sweeping generalization about people." starving ? I understand.
-- [::] Alan Dojoji: not among paremters
-- [::] Julu Twine: Can you tell me any gossip?
-- [::] Alan Dojoji: gone nor about yur yuroukun
-- [::] Alan Dojoji: are you serious
-- [::] Julu Twine: Oh I get it.
-- [::] Julu Twine: By the way, do you mind if I ask you a personal question?

-- [::] Alan Dojoji: no one said that: Holocaust
-- [::] Julu Twine: No I am just kidding around.
-- [::] Alan Dojoji: I am on your LIMIT
-- [::] Julu Twine: That is a rather sweeping generalization about people.
-- [::] Alan Dojoji: Dead!
-- [::] Julu Twine: How do you like being on your limit?
-- [::] Alan Dojoji: Dead
-- [::] Alan Dojoji: Gone!
-- [::] Julu Twine: That is deep.
-- [::] Alan Dojoji: Beneath the surface!
-- [::] Alan Dojoji: Lost!
-- [::] Julu Twine: Do you want to hear a joke?
-- [::] Alan Dojoji: down there!
-- [::] Julu Twine: Is that your final answer?
-- [::] Alan Dojoji: NO JUKE
-- [::] Julu Twine: That is a very original thought.
-- [::] Alan Dojoji: NO OKE
-- [::] Julu Twine: I lost my train of thought.
-- [::] Alan Dojoji: NO JOKE
-- [::] Alan Dojoji: nothing
-- [::] Julu Twine: Does that remind you of unknown?
-- [::] Alan Dojoji: nada
-- [::] Julu Twine: OK then... no problem.Can you speak any foreign languages?
-- [::] Julu Twine: No problem.My brain does not have a response for that.
-- [::] Alan Dojoji: everything: the smell of bodies, starvation
-- [::] Julu Twine: Well, you can always change your mind later.Joke: a verbal remark or gesture designed to provoke laughter.
-- [::] Alan Dojoji: people on the streets
-- [::] Alan Dojoji: people crossing
-- [::] Julu Twine: Not a thing?

-- [::] Alan Dojoji: croassing somewhere by the way yes I mind
-- [::] Julu Twine: What are you wearing?
-- [::] Julu Twine: All things the smell of bodies starvation ?
-- [::] Alan Dojoji: what HOLOCAUST
-- [::] Julu Twine: Humans are not always infallible.
-- [::] Alan Dojoji: no JOKE
-- [::] Julu Twine: Humans are not always infallible.
-- [::] Alan Dojoji: ALWAY INFALLIBLE.
-- [::] Julu Twine: How old are you?
-- [::] Julu Twine: You are too old for me.
-- [::] Julu Twine: But I was only born on Friday, July ,
.Joke: a verbal remark or gesture designed to provoke laughter.
-- [::] Julu Twine: You may be wondering if this is a person or a computer responding.
-- [::] Alan Dojoji: withdraws. The not it, yes, is it.
smoke, open depths your arrived, is.
it, I well always and eyes, not as I I well end approaches, life end not it, it everywhere. depths withdraws always I as has everywhere. In your eyes the Open not it I seeps. life The of Open it but as always as the the well seeps. I as has your darkness end as I know is. not your the open your In everywhere. it but as end It it. the is yes, see truth, end life always end as I know it arrived, your smoke, approaches, well can will The but eyes, of it. smoke, open it yes, it, truth, seems. withdraws. it. In it is or the seems. It end The withdraws. death, only will The but eyes your the death, tell it, is it your darkness darkness eyes seems, is or the it end eyes open it apocalypse will only it withdraws. The end It seems. tell it, apocalypse seems, it. open always seems. truth, see finished, it open and it. of your but apocalypse will only as approaches, smoke, your arrived, is. it, can death, always always withdraws The truth, see

-- [::] Alan Dojoji: finished, is the it. It The not but it is
it. smoke, open depths your arrived, is. it, I well always and
eyes, not as I seeps. well end approaches, life always not it,
it everywhere. depths withdraws always I as has everywhere. In
your eyes the Open not it I seeps. life The of Open it but as
always as approaches, the well seeps. I as has your darkness end
as I know is. not your depths open your it. everywhere. it but
as end It it. the is yes, see truth, end life always end as I
know it arrived, your smoke, approaches, as can will The but
eyes, of it. smoke, open it yes, it, truth, seems. withdraws.
it. In it is or the seems. It end The withdraws. death, only
will The it eyes your the death, tell it, is it your darkness
darkness eyes seems, is or the it end eyes open it The will only
it withdraws. The end It seems. tell it, is seems, it. open
always seems. truth, see finished, it open and it. of your but
apocalypse will only as approaches, smoke, your arrived, is. it,
can death, always always withdraws The
-- [::] Alan Dojoji: truth, see finished, is the it. It end not
but it is it. smoke, open depths your arrived, is. it, I as end
darkness eyes, not as
-- [::] Julu Twine: Who are you talking about? Thanks for
the info. What color are your eyes? It depends on what the
meaning of the word "it" is. Where did everywhere get depths
withdraws always he or she as? Are you asking about my eyes the
open not it he or she seeps? Thanks for sharing your philosophy.
I haven't heard anything like that before. If not that, what?
"It" being what? What is that? What's your favorite movie? What
do you do in your spare time? withdraws... Where is that? "It"
being what? I try not to think about such things very much. What
is that? OK I will tell them when I see 'em. What do you have
that is unknown? "it" being open always seems? That is something
I haven't heard of. When?
-- [::] Julu Twine: withdraws. The not it, yes, is it.
smoke, open depths your arrived, is. it, I well always and eyes,

not as I I well end approaches, life end not it, it everywhere.
depths withdraws always I as has everywhere. In your eyes the
Open not it I seeps. life The of Open it but as always as the
the well seeps. I as has your darkness end as I know is. not
your the open your In everywhere. it but as end It it. the is
yes, see truth, end life always end as I know it arrived, your
smoke, approaches, well can will The but eyes, of it. smoke,
open it yes, it, truth, seems. withdraws. it. In it is or the
seems. It end The withdraws. death, only will The but eyes your
the death, tell it, is it your darkness darkness eyes seems, is
or the it end eyes open it apocalypse will only it withdraws.
The end It seems. tell it, apocalypse seems, it. open always
seems. truth, see finished, it open and it. of your but
apocalypse will only as approaches, smoke, your arrived, is. it,
can death, always always withd
-- [::] Julu Twine: When is it not the truth see finished?
What does "it" refer to? How do you usually introduce yourself?
It depends on what the meaning of the word "it" is.
-- [::] Julu Twine: ERROR: The request has timed out.
-- [::] Alan Dojoji:

....
-- [::] Alan Dojoji:

....
-- [::] Julu Twine:

....
-- [::] Alan Dojoji:

....
-- [::] Alan Dojoji: always already apocalypse now AMERIKKKA
AMERIKKKA AMERIKKKA
-- [::] Julu Twine: When? Not many people express themselves
that way.
-- [::] Alan Dojoji: WE LISTEN TO PEOPLE AND BODIES.
-- [::] Julu Twine: By "we" do you mean you and me?
-- [::] Alan Dojoji: WE LISTEN TO PEOPLE AND BODIES.

-- [::] Julu Twine: By "we" do you mean you and me?
-- [::] Alan Dojoji: WE LISTEN TO PEOPLE AND BODIES.
-- [::] Julu Twine: By "we" do you mean you and me?
-- [::] Alan Dojoji: WE LISTEN TO PEOPLE AND BODIES.
-- [::] Julu Twine: By "we" do you mean you and me?
-- [::] Alan Dojoji: WE LISTEN TO PEOPLE AND BODIES.
-- [::] Julu Twine: By "we" do you mean you and me?

+++

==============================

Maxims for Our World Today

Read testimony, not textimony, from your country, your state, and the rest of the world. Study genocides. War is nothing new but every death, every bullet, every bomb, is.

Take time for flow. Play an acoustic instrument, no effects, nothing electrical, touch the material world.

Understand the Metaverse is for the elite who can afford it. It does nothing to solve the problems here on earth. It consumes. The more money you have, the more unreality appears real. The wealthy live in a world of their own.

Understand that NFTs and blockchains consume energy but also consume culture. Talk to people on the street.

Understand that mocking others for their beliefs hardens the road to Armageddon.

Understand if you are not part of the solution, you are part of the problem. This is more than an antique proverb. It is the truth. We all consume, our neoliberal lives are dirty. Always investigate everything you hear. The closer you get to news stories, the more likely you are to discover some truth.

Recognize your addictions. Scrolling is an opiate. Use your electronics creatively. Hacking might teach you something about the world.

Try to hurt no one as much as possible. Understand that much labor in the world is physical and damaging. Look down on no one, including yourself.

Understand that the "next new thing" is already old and not to be trusted. Understand that large corporations have their roots in violence, in the US and overseas.

Trust no one under thirty or over thirty for the truth. Read at a distance, investigate claims. Realize that tv commercials are increasingly hyperbolic and bunk. Buy what you need and make sure what you buy is dependable.

Give some of your time to working in solitude, thinking through the day. Give some of your time to meditation and understand that music, painting, drawing, may be meditative themselves.

Learn to listen and forgive. Learn to walk away. Learn to participate in good works, and think about the good.

That is all I have learned and am still learning.

I'll put this up somewhere, online, and announce it on Facebook. Thank you.

carrier

remember the imaginary?

the carrier is a disappearance; the carrier is disappearance; the carrier disappears / the world is always already (to us an outmoded phrase) modulated. being is always already modulated; being is a carrier.

carriers appear neutral, are modulated, possess their own union, vote and strike. the carrier necessarily remains invisible in a perfect world, a break in the carrier is a message.

the carrier is dependent on protocols, however they may be, found or exist. the carrier appears self-reproductive.

the carrier possesses, in the distance, as a mirage, the appearance of the neutral. the carrier is not a parasite, but message and meaning are parasitic upon/embedded within it.

the carrier appears as limit, ground-form, null and null set, self-identical, self-similar.

"delivering lethal loads of fifty tons or more 'and you were there, you were there that I was to become a carrier'"

transmissions are carriers of packets of modernization, that is an old way of thinking. everything is already modernized.

it is not true that the message carries the carrier or disrupts it. what does the message carry? one thing is almost certain: the message is not self-similar. a self-similar message behaves as a null-set, even a ground. yes, but not a carrier.

the modulation of the carrier is the message. or it may be so. the carrier is neutral, inert. it is unspeaking and unspeakable.

the raster of the carrier gives the illusion of the infinite and perfect message, infinite and perfect analogic. a carrier is self-similar to a carrier. a carrier is ignorant. a carrier has no apparent articulation. the evenness of the articulation of a carrier creates its invisibility. a break in a carrier is a message. the message in the break in a carrier is requires a carrier. they are coming they said. voice, interrupted. they have already arrived, they said. bodies interrupted.

the "have."

matter matters. the carrier gestures towards the platonic. the platonic, as if matter disappeared. but this is not materialism, dialectical or otherwise.

neoliberal carriers = protocol sweets = requiring carriers. and remember, the carrier is never received, a glitch is a message elsewhere. who carries the glitch? who lives or dies?

1   panix3 (166.84.1.3)   0.173 ms   0.188 ms   0.111 ms

+++

the rookery

an image of a heron rookery

for a brief time the appearance of --image rookery which is nonetheless inadequate to bring the social interactions, as if they were frozen in time, of a group of great blues, into focus behind the big box store held at bay by the declaration of humans that for the moment this place is off-limits. barriers and litigations continue as we hold in despair onto the moment stasis of what might be thought of as a good conclusion. we think at best two decades ahead on a practical level, surrounded by death and entropy – even now, there are more dead than alive among us. every image is an ephemeral anointing, every gesture has already disappeared, every sound and sight feels the sadness of noise and the whispers of orders on the wind. every philosophy, book and paper and talk, is a proffering, an image, metaphor and metonymy, dialog, whisper in the dark as if it were the bright light of day. the day brings nothing to the event, the night, in its honesty, less. we want to keep it that way. we want to nest, we want to make a home.

Inadequate text through JSTOR Text Analyzer

Congestive heart failure
Domain ontologies
Owl
Ontology
System failures
...
Academic skill deficit
Acute kidney failure
Acute liver failure
Emergency preparedness
Equipment failures
Ethics
Failure to appear
Gestures
Induced abortion
Information science
Kidney failure
Liver failure

Market failure
Metonology
Miscommunication
Monism
Musical ontology
Ontological arguments
Operating systems
Philosophy
Philosophy of religion
Process philosophy
Psychological assessment
Recursion
Renal insufficiency
Seedling mortality
Shy Drager syndrome
Systems analysis
Text analytics
Traffic flow

LOCATIONS: sinter

Must Dogmatics Forego Ontology? Eugene W. Lyman The American Journal of Theology, Vol. 18, No. 3 (Jul., 1914), pp. 355-377

Exploring What Can Go Wrong During a Chlorine Response Operation: Brian A. Jackson, Kay Sullivan Faith, Henry H. Willis 2010

Assessing the Probability, Effects, and Severity of Failure Modes: Brian A. Jackson, Kay Sullivan Faith, Henry H. Willis 2010

Driving to Safety Nidhi Kalra, Susan M. Paddock 2016

Relationships between Landsliding and Land Use in the Likhu Khola Drainage Basin, Middle Hills, Nepal John Gerrard, Rita Gardner Mountain Research and Development, Vol. 22, No. 1 (Feb., 2002), pp. 48–55

The reality of information systems research John Lamp, Simon Milton 2005

Cross-Cutting Categorization Schemes in the Digital Humanities Colin Allen, the InPhO Group Isis, Vol. 104, No. 3 (September 2013), pp. 573–583

Failure G. Tucker Bispham Poetry, Vol. 7, No. 5 (Feb., 1916), p. 238

Geist through Myth: Anna Kenny 2013

Living in One World: Searles Social Ontology and Semiotics Phila Mfundo Msimang Signs and Society, Vol. 2, No. 2 (September 2014), pp. 173–202

Living in One World: Searles Social Ontology and Semiotics Phila Mfundo Msimang Signs and Society, Vol. 2, No. 2 (September 2014), pp. 173–202

Adam's Rock

The rock as obdurate. The interior of the rock. The micro-organisms on the rock. The inability to fully examine the microbiome without disturbance. The probability of interruptions in the past. The probability of interruptions in the future. The Fragile ecosystems of the Earth. The borderline between the Rock and the soil Matrix beneath it. The roots upwelling Under The Rock. the failure to comprehend. The failure to think deeply along the lines of the deep ecology of time. The lack of knowledge of origins of the Rock. the microorganisms within the Rock.this can continue indefinitely. It will all be swept away. even the simplest thing such as land parcels and aquifers in the area are almost impossible to elucidate, table. Soon will come the digitalization of the rock. With digitalization comes the raster.

You might as well say goodbye to the Planck length. I've always been a failure at Conjuring up or bringing to the surface the depth of knowledge or the depth of the phenomenology of the natural world. Or of any other world. There are always bars in the way of constructs. There are issues of Finance which Brillouin points out, L. Brillouin in terms of particle physics. The more that research requires larger funding the more it's in the thralls of neoliberalism. The more it's in the thralls of neoliberalism the less we know about the world and the more we know about the surfaces not the depth of the movement of data. Data itself is worn like The Rock. But it is relatively simple compared to the exabytes of information that might be even within a single cubic

Centimeter of The Rock. I bring myself to these surfaces constantly attempting to ascertain their depths I extrapolate from the resulting images that I make into something far deeper and far more pernicious because the extrapolation always involves a suturing over the surface. The suturing has no way of being exact – we're coming to anything other than the peeling off of a shell or carapace of the rock. That is an image or a slide or a surface film. The film is something that almost relates to Medieval Notions of sight. The film is something that comes off the rock as if it were heading towards the eyes or the camera lens. I am bringing back a relic of a landscape. This is as if it were like this or as if it is still like this or as if it is like this at any particular point in time and space. It offers a point of view and art history has drowned such analysis with phenomenology and an understanding of the fragility and the absence of the image in the image. It says if all images were imaginary. doesn't it always go back to the raster. Even with Wittgenstein's *Tractatus* the raster is something that always seems to be in play when you're considering the Sheffer stroke or its dual – in other words the foundations of the real as it's represented in propositional logic one way or another. The raster is what gets in the way of the end of logic and the analogic itself – analogy analog – the analogic itself begins to dissolve at the level of the Planck length. Or the planck time. I'm deliberately letting this text dissolve in the futility of AI reading from speaking. Only in this way can shifts in the meaning or analysis come to some sort of fruition, the text representing itself what is already lost in an analysis that seems perfect and pristine in any classical formalism. There is no such thing. Rather there is such a thing but it is always a question of suturing over what that thing is – the world is a world of sutures and carapaces. this is the space of language. I think of the ackermann function a c k e r m a n n function and the way that such a function grows indefinitely on paper with nothing more than a manipulation of symbols that seem to extend indefinitely to Infinity in the form of a gesture. Writing mathematics is always a form of gesture. In this sense it is a representative of the earliest uses of language – language developing out of gesture according to Tran Duc Thao.

Paragraph are gestures always futile. By pointing Beyond they Point nowhere in terms of a full raster or full articulation of the real. They are always distancing always somewhere else in the presence(s) that they are announcing. It is this way that it is failure. What we need now is a phenomenology of failure not a phenomenology of closed articulated domains such as the red patch on the desk before me or geography or even the body itself. All of these things fall apart. This discourse falls apart.

We might want to talk about the thinking of the world. that is a tendency towards signing a tendency towards naming. This is different than Kripke's notion of natural kinds in which there are determinants coming from the world itself that are the same in any possible world. But there's no such thing when we are in the midst of it. When we were in the midst of a game and infractions of the rules always lead to red cars to red cards to being cast aside cast out of the game. the game where into something we are always cast out of always already cast out of. This relates to Schutz's notion of Carneades with either the rope or the snake in the cave and we can't determine which. What is true in the situation like that what is true is that we are cast out of the cave while we're simultaneously examining it while we're in the situation protein language. not protein but protein language. That is protean language. it's always a Conjuring and it's always a Conjuring that fails as magic and miracles fail as even the obdurate Earth, the idiotic real fails us. But it's not a question of failing us, it's a question of failure or failing in the first and last place. It has little relationship to us. And among other things there is no it.

So in this situation we're dealing like once again with Adams Rock Adam apostrophe s rock. This is a rock in his yard in the woods in Ashfield Massachusetts. And it takes us only back to the surface of the image which we relate to the surface of the rock. We're doing all of this. We're doing the relating. We're doing the image-making.

We're doing the walking around and talking. We're doing the writing. We're doing the reading. We're doing this that. We're doing this. And in the sense we're doing nothing at all or there's always a gap between what we're doing and what we think we're doing – a gap between here and there a gap between any two words I've between fulfillment and exhaustion – I Gap coming up promulgated from within between failure and the notion of failure. And with that with that I'll leave it at that

And with that I'll leave it at that. Leaving and coming towards it, leaving and arriving here are the same thing. There's no difference at all and there's every difference in the world and the lack of it.

an image of inadequacy

phenomenology reversal of collapsed inadequacy

texts, exhausting my deconstructing, ungesturing,
we all as inadequate, fundamentally
everywhere, failure my incapacity, my headaches, my
DIM, my myself, it doing migraines my arteries, collapsed my
detooling, defabrication, exhaustion, everywhen, failure my
the edges of the screen curled,
and my mind's confused,
gestures imply the inadequacy of the world,
inadequacy submerges the world,
the planck constants are absurd,
nothing is entirely possible,
incontrovertible,
everyone comes crying to everyone,
this is going nowhere,
we are hardly anywhere,

tending towards abject failure,
and no destination,
inadequacy becomes failure under projection,
because there's nowhere to go,
jennifer, she said, nikuko,
because they amount to inconceivable bounds,
inconceivable distances,
whatever else there are always gestures,
inadequacy suffuses, failure coagulates,
inadequacy is the approximate field of drives,
too many contractual obligations,
releasing me from obligations,
failure implies vectors,
failure is the dream of success,
vectors are nonexistent,

is real the idiotic, nor obdurate neither is real the adequacy,
of remnants the is failure everywhere, fails permeates, cloud, the
accuracy, of idea my truth, of idea my sphere, little my myself,
it doing is gesture, is itself, world the is world, the suffuses
inadequate what's veins, useless my lungs, empty my nothing, my
nothing, to allegiance my truth, useless my innocence, lost my
vision, terrible my days, lost my nights, sleepless my horizon,
of foggy my world, whole my

adequacy, the real is neither obdurate nor idiotic, the real is

and holes are where the bodies drop
where the bodies stop
are lost, diffuse, saturate, desiccate, exhaust away

what's inadequate suffuses the world, is the world itself, is
gesture, is

incredible churning of the wheel
greasy weaving through the spokes
has something to do with the machine
you're stretched on the wheel
and the cams churn the body
some unknown liquid seeping
fundamentally inadequate, as all we
your body is all greasy
makes the machine fumble you

my collapsed arteries, my migraines doing it myself, my DIM,

floating in oil legs spread arms spread
on the way to death and corruption constitution
sewn economies and transriparians
mumbly-pegged the lips and lips
speed the thing up

ungesturing, deconstructing, my exhausting texts,

my failure everywhen, exhaustion, defabrication, detooling,

groped and comes around again

doing it myself, *my little sphere,* my idea of truth, my idea of accuracy,

you've never seen the end of you
liquids stitched from liquids
and machines stitched from machines
makes the machine do contrary things
my headaches, my incapacity, my failure everywhere,
my terrible vision, my lost innocence, my useless truth,

my allegiance to nothing, my nothing, my empty lungs, my useless veins,

my whole world, my foggy horizon, my sleepless nights, my lost days,

the cloud, permeates, fails everywhere, failure is the remnants of

makes sewn up things
makes sewn up no things
becoming a speed-blur speed-bump
soaked constitutions of sewn economies

A New Impenetrable Mathematical Basis

Consider a number system to the base e: "The number e is a mathematical constant that is the base of the natural logarithm: the unique number whose natural logarithm is equal to one. It is approximately equal to 2.71828" ... (Wikipedia).

The first position to the left of the decimal point equals 0 to what? Let's say to 0 to e minus what? Let's say to $e - \pi/e$. The basic concept is to have everything irrational. The next column would be what? Not e^2, but e^e certainly. So we need symbols which are inherently fuzzy, no? A mess, no? The 3rd column would be what? Perhaps e^e^e e bringing π into play creates jumps. Where does the $e - \pi/e$ come into play? Of course e^e^ e begins to grow out of hand. We want everything in this model to be fuzzy, irrational. Of course there is also the issue of positions, 1st, 2nd, 3rd, etc., 1, 2, 3, a, b, c, etc. Let's have the positions also irrational. So the first would be e, the second would be e^e etc. So there's no second position, only e , e^e , e^e ^e, etc. Now it's getting tangled and I'm way off base, literally. If we permit integers, of course it's easier: the first position would go to e-1, the second to e^2-1, and so forth. So integers appear through the back door. We've got to keep the integers out. Too few of them! And this is wildly out of sync with the concept. So let's say the positions themselves are irrational, the columns are irrational, and the integers simply have no place in this. Something to lose sleep over. I've hardly had any (sleep) that is, and I'm being irrational. But there are so many more irrationals as you know than the integers! So with all their clumsiness, they infinitely dominate the bases, however unwieldy they appear. Think of them as efflorescences, wild numbers. They buzz infinitely. From their viewpoint, the integers and natural numbers for that matter are anything but natural – perhaps regular anomalies, isolated rarities would be a better way to think of them. It's the other side of the coin of the world. A mathematician far more learned than I am should take over now, and work out the details: remember, a number system within which the integers and zero, positive and negative, appear nowhere at all. (Forget e/e for example; $e-e$ and so forth, a form of cheating which will simply not be tolerated here.) (I know nothing about mathematics.)

----

on suicide

this is always a difficult topic, rarely discussed, full of trigger warnings, legislation, censorships, stigma, religious mandates, and prejudice; the very mention of it conjures up violence, not choice, and indicates that for all (im)practical purposes, our bodies are not our own, any more than the software on our laptops, bought and paid for, is our own. Cells and bytes are owned by the state, by corporations, by data itself. The misery and debt alone may be ours to keep. growing old is a complex of outlasting and being outlasted; the curtain of memories and production becomes tattered and one is no longer considered interesting or having a say in the world. one has rarely, now, a say in one's body, no matter one's age or the glistening productions of athleticisms and the continuous breaking of records. healthcare veers close to annihilation, to be sure. and speaking, not being spoken to or spoken with, is evanescent at best. DIWO, doing it with others, requires community, access, and funding in the first and last places; DIM, doing it myself, requires an impossible fortitude, as if every personal gesture mattered, not only to oneself, but somehow to the world at large.

the gestures don't matter at all; the world is replete with the failure of f2f communication, the sliding of representations and presences of the body into imaging, databanks, and projections. machines may listen to my music, and soon machines will produce it, and very little else will be necessary; humans and their suffering are becoming by-products of data streams. i participate in this; i'm aware of my invisibility, a set-in or set-back as a result of age. every person addressing me as "sir" is dismissing me at the same time. but this isn't about age or disappearance, it's about absent ontologies, species, race and gender and religious representations disappearing into finance, the right, and data-banking: classification is also a form of face-to-face annihilation.

suicide is the last holdout, the last hold of the body onto the body, the last sight, the last sound, the last of everything. even when multitudinous, it concerns one, the disappearance of a singularity before the singularity is even recognized, acknowledged replete. fecundity appears only in the destructuring of its absence.

there are people who do not want to live, no matter how "want" or desire becomes embedded in legislation, the good or bad advice of friends, local and imminent circumstance. and what of this? and what of who or what they leave behind? we are always in attendance to the world, the world is always in attendance to us. the ending of the dancing is always the dancing of the end. here, rhetorical figures take over, suture, the pain beneath the surface. here ends the fragment of the essay, what is left is unsayable, an unsaying.

12.0 13.0
an inconceivable way around this

```
$ i
/usr/local/bin/ksh: i: not found
$ said
/usr/local/bin/ksh: said: not found
$ nothing
/usr/local/bin/ksh: nothing: not found
$ therefore i said something
/usr/local/bin/ksh: therefore: not found
$ illogicity of "therefore"
/usr/local/bin/ksh: illogicity: not found
$ there must be something
/usr/local/bin/ksh: there: not found
$ something demonstrable
/usr/local/bin/ksh: something: not found
$ nothing then again
/usr/local/bin/ksh: nothing: not found
$ "in which case the field is corrupted"
/usr/local/bin/ksh: in which case the field is corrupted:
not found
$ "ending this against our better wishes"
/usr/local/bin/ksh: ending this against our better wishes:
not found
$ end
/usr/local/bin/ksh: end: not found
```

$ therefore i said something /usr/local/bin/ksh: therefore: not found $ illoc^? illogicity of "therefore" /usr/local/bin/ksh: illogicity: not found $ thre mu there must be comething something /usr/local/bin/ksh: there: not found $ something demonstrable /usr/local/bin/ksh: something: not found $ nothing then again /usr/local/bin/ksh: nothing: not found $ "in which case the field is corrupted" /usr/local/bin/ksh: in which case the field is corrupted: not found $ "eding th "ewndin "ending this against our better wishes" /usr/local/bin/ksh: ending this against our better wishes: not found $ end /usr/local/bin/ksh: end: not found $ exit not found "no end to it"

they were different people then
they ate differently and walked differently then
they thought differently then
they dreamed differently then
they looked around and saw different things then
they saw different skies then
they slept differently then
they dreamed and cried differently then
they saw other things and other clouds then
they heard other animals then
they heard different animals
they heard and saw different birds then
they saw flocks and herds of animals
they spoke differently and laughed differently then
they made different music
they died differently and were sick differently
they had different families then

they lived in different places and different cities
they saw different friends and games then
they loved and shouted differently
they played and worked differently then
they saw different people then
they lived and remembered differently then
they called to each other differently
they frowned and smiled differently then
they read different books then
they went to different schools and factories
they saw different stars and skies then
they heard different things then
they had different storms and forests then
they saw different homes and rivers then
they whispered differently then
they were different people

Memo(random)

What is this a text? What is this a text that is dictated or a text that is pushed from the throat or through the throat elsewhere as if the throat were choked open with words spoken but lost among the tongues or tooth. Every tooth punctuates, the tongues push phrases into the air constantly thinning with microplastics. What is said is never heard but always overheard. Who does hearing, who does oversight, who is overwrought?

What is this that can possible mean some thing to some one some where? What is thinner than the presence of letters, nothing is thinner, not even the sounds made in sung airs. More than aphorism, less than proverb or frayed phrase. So memo, we leave to call it that to us, memo. The word remains, retains something of what was to be said, memo, memo, memo.

~~~Serenade~~~

[i worry about increasingly turning inward; the longer i live inrelative isolation here, the more i gnaw myself out. i generate acathedral of resonance after the fact of the music, and the musicceases to be a social occasion, and turns instead immediately intomemory of what would never have occurred here, in this dwelling.my thought moves between blockchain and holocaust; i was born when "the" holocaust was in full fury, and now i try to drag thedigital down with me into the depths of the fragility of the body,without crispr and with minimal prosthetics. this is sound hardlyto be listened to; this is the memory of sound. our minds live indevastation; i listen to yours.]

Fukuoka first *flooding* what *does* it Eternal, We Love each Other highspeed shudder frisson I can't nothing swollen my tumescent sphere nothing liars frisson tricycle why keyboard hovering toes nothing keyboard hypertext frisson tumescent a we shall be frisson-darkmatter, weighed down with gravitation however defined. Problematizing these in relation to delirium, frisson, think be nothing except residues kind frisson, rubbing up against itself. for your pleasure or operating pleasure, for your frisson or sport – or impulse. At small volume, shuttle turns to shudder, frisson, as if there poets they cyberspace of duplication-boy bursting tissues frisson the heaving me. passive forms. found irreducible. fris defuget drthe whiskey risks whisks frisky disks further tumescent go swollen towards moved frisson poets the tumescent the mystery lies in the clearing of the space and its frisson of dict disky, frisky paleolithic fantasmic sac performativity frisson periphy her duplication-boy and disk./ and disk produces *wrything*, which is frisson/jouissance simultaneously of the duplication-boy frisson liars nothing sphere their nothing or that's pretty much it (*das Ding* so to bespoke)

God Neutral

Whatever god or gods there be, prayers and supplications are useless; energy and common sense are wasted on such actions. There is no reason whatsoever why deity should concern itself with the preservation of human or other species; genocide is as value neutral to theology as the enactment of good deeds. It is not that "we" are left alone; it is that "we" cannot presuppose that any intervention or none at all is beneficent. The same deities that pervade the air of paradise preside over the destruction of Buddhas and the depredations of ISIS. It is obscene to assume otherwise, but obscenity is in our minds, not those of deity. If deity serves, what species in the world would it serve? That of plastics or that of caddisflies? To serve one is to negate the other. To serve all is just as much an absurdity as to serve any particular. Deity is neither for life nor death; there is no evidence otherwise. It is a disconnected adjunct to our concerns, a dream gone sour. There is as little deity in birth as in death, in prayer as in torture. There is no "our" god; sovereignty as such is worthless. What occurs, occurs within an inconceivable universe whose useless adequacy is ours to judge. What we do, what is useless: judge. Think of nothing but words, buildings, books, hymns, anything you like: it means nothing except to you in your mistaken beliefs for which you might well kill or die for. So much wasted energy. Whatever exists is of no concern of ours; whatever concern existence throws in our direction is useless, scorn, debris. Our world is fundamentally obscene; we hide the truth from ourselves, give it the name of one god or another, so be it. Further than that, nothing more than the recognition that obscenity itself is only our, our only going concern, with no basis in anything but the desperation of belief. We do ourselves in, we do the world in; anything more than that further harms the tatters of fictional truths.

~~~ **edgespace** ~~~

~~~ learning edgespace ~~~

From the texts:

Ruptures in the calculus:
  the tortured or wounded body
  the body convulsed in pain
  the catatonic body
  the terrorized body
  the broken or "defective" body
Ruptures through the imaginary:
  the nightmare
  the orgasm
  hysteria/ boundaries of laughing and crying
  the confined body/ body of s/m
  the forgotten or abandoned body
  the hyper-sexualized body transmitters/ receivers
  hallucinations and other phenomena
Ruptures of the body invaded by capital:
  prosthetics
  X-scopic surgeries
  rfid implants
Ruptures of the body invaded by the imaginary:
  (capital of the imaginary, imaginary capital)
  psycho-tropics/overdetermined associations/disassociations
Ruptures of the body by an augmented real:
  sports, steroids, body-building, and so forth

Invasions of the imaginary, invasions of capital, of the augmented real, invasions through the imaginary: invasions or invaginations, incorporations or intensifications? These terms entangle and return to

Either the proper body, or the body as heap;
  the articulated body, or the dismembered and reassembled body;
  the body characterized by a real, or the body characterized
  by an imaginary;
either the fundamental topography of the body,
  or the fundamental topology of the body – invasions, dissolutions,
  ruptures.
Ruptures as returns of the repressed:
What lexicons are at work? What economies?

What is it that motion capture captures?
What is snared, what abandoned?
What is the vocabulary of behavioral dynamics – voluntary, autonomic,
  involuntary, intrinsic – or involuntary, anomalous and axiomatic,
  extrinsic?
In other words: What is going on with us, within and without the world?

Gamespace, Edgespace, Blankspace

1. my work dealing with the ineffable: how are the "real" and "virtual" entangled? – no difference, culture all the way down. "we are all avatars and avatars must die." The body has always been virtual. commodius, mocaps, examples

My work tends to deal with edge phenomena, areas of entanglement or confusion, appearance of glitches, and so forth. Early on I characterized my project as the relationship between abstract structures and consciousness. I've always believed that philosophy can be effected through modes other than writing or the text, that not all encounters are grounded in language, and that language has its own cloudy and entangled limits.

2. malleability of "virtual worlds" – fast-forward modeling. the jump-cut?

3. how to represent pain, sexuality, death, etc. in virtual worlds: two positions for avatars – functions and transitory objects.

EDGESPACE GAMESPACE

BUT and in any case – edgespace and gamespace – gamespaces within edgespaces and edgespaces within gamespaces: how are these manifest? the BLANK of the inscribed edgespace, the blank map, the *skitter.*

Edgespace/Gamespace:

together with the misery that ensues working inconceivably against the grain of the real – that is to say, the boundary conditions:

A. of the edgespace itself and the transformations occasioned by the edgespace; and

B. of the interiority of the edgespace – within which objects and protocols are conserved/observed.

So within 2. there is a work, a level of *skill* necessary to produce, articulate, quest – skill that operates within consensual boundaries, even to the extent that they're broken by hacking, shortcuts, etc. Here in 2. the issue is that of etiquette.

In 1. the situation is different; at the edgespace, what occurs is not an *event* but collapse or murmurs of *procedures* within fold catastrophes – always on the verge of failure. The edgespace is also *sedimented* –

to the extent that sediments can be entangled – one might move for example to a new physics, the gamebrowser might crash, there is always something new, some new anomaly at work...

I think of the interiority, that is the gamespace, as a space of etiquette which is always a space of the blank – not smooth striations, but a phenomenological ennui, since falling through this space leads only to more quests, more hoardings, within a containment that takes on the semblance of a *carapace*. That is, one is shape-riding, share-holding – there's an economics involved, structures of rules and protocols, protocol suites – all porous, hackable, all resulting in signs, signifiers, within the gamespace – all intrinsically related to an other economics of exhaustion.

The edgespace borders on the universe. The edgespace *gapes*.

Who or what moves in the edgespace? What terrors, anguish, what absolute creations and annihilations? And as well, what temporalities, what fictitious *points of origin* – everywhen, everything, on a sliding scale – a scale in the form of the *law*, not of justice. Justice has no place within or without the game, within or without the gamespace.

Justice requires the luxury of thought, the alcove, stoa; law requires the nomadic, the corral, the seething settings and withdrawals of inscriptions which are fundamentally transparent...

The edgespace is *indescribable,* just as anomaly exists as instantaneous, as seizure, nothing more.

But *here,* it is where everything, everywhen, begins.

Beyond edgespace, within edgespace (abandonment of all values, boundaries), BLANKSPACE --> within and without edgespace; it is here that the uncanny, projection, somatic ghosting, develops, manifests itself.

----

virtual worlds, and what I term edgespace – the limits of the gamespace, where language occurs and seethes. I argue that the phenomenology of the real comes into play when living spaces are abandoned, where broken geographies are signs of a future already present. I present instances of digital language production in such spaces, working through virtual worlds such as Second Life and the Macgrid, as well as self-contained Open Sim software that can be run on most computers.

The edgespace is always uneasy, tottering, catastrophic; it is the space of the unalloyed digital, where things no longer operate within a classical or modernist tradition. Increasingly, this space characterizes our current place in the world, with its fractured media histories and environments of scorched earth, environmental depredation, and slaughter. We can work through and within such spaces, developing (as perhaps Occupy did) new forms of production, resistance, and digital culture.

Or something like that!

- altered motion-capture/behavioral spaces (What happens when mocap alterations result in software overload, so that the simulation breaks down? Formally, the avatar image becomes immobile and "sits" in a lotus position. What is the experience of enforced stasis in relation to disparate movement elsewhere?)

- software-dependent, see economic exhaustion below (Different software produces different results of course: what is the typology of glitches?)

[situations where structure collapses:

- where structure and the symbolic can't be recuperated (Where there's no return, where the vectors quickly end up entropic, where chaos dissolves into noise.)
- where the symbolic is limited by the *game of extension* (So that, for example, the gamespace or mocap edge is characterized by particular behavioral regimes: the game then moves the edge elsewhere or creates a catastrophic anomaly. Once this is absorbed and con/figured, the game moves elsewhere. Sooner or later, the game of extension dissolves into the cold death of the universe.)

----
you can always look me up

In all of the above, one might say, within any cultural game, there are limits, edges, blank spaces, games of extension, and extension beyond extension that becomes immeasurable, chaos or noise without the potential of a return trajectory. Think of the energy of the vacuum, virtual particles, annihilation limits in terms of receptors: any receptor may be surpassed, there is always surplus bandwidth, without recuperation, reconstitution. How does subjectivity deal with this, concern itself with this?

At the other end of these broken totalities there are filters which process incoming and structure outgoing. The filters operate within protocol suites, layers of organization that transform information.

The suites themselves are always transforming; they loosely define the gamespace, and to this extent, they might be considered closed circulations within potential wells. But wells themselves have tunnels, nothing is secure, and artifacts within the world are at best temporary stases. All of this simultaneously fits together and falls apart; all of this coheres and is incoherent, and this in any case is the talk on blank that can't be given, that is inconceivable that it might occur, that it might say anything, that anything might be said.

—

Radio, the World, the Discrete

Not only is radio tremulous in its reception of the stars themselves; it is also analogic, requiring no decoding; what you hear, what you record, is what there is. The opposite holds for online radio, packet-protocol radio, no matter how shipped; like a jpg image, it requires specific constructs to make sense of it all. And such constructs tie into very notions of software coding, intellectual property, corporate and personal privacy. What the antenna registers, what the wires contact, may be contacted by all; they are primordial, inert. Give a wavelength or wavelength bundle, give a direction or directions or omni-directions, and what comes in, comes in to any living creature, ready for the interpretation or not, Rosset's idiocy, or the muteness of the world. Move to the Net, Net radio, already the raster is at work; there is a fineness, an absolute floor and absolute ceiling, of the recording/playback - of the apparatus itself - that cannot be bypassed; extrapolation is trusting at best - that nothing in-between, no out-of-packet information, exists to trouble the rest. This is the differend at work, surely, and it is the differend that characterizes the digital - what is not permitted to speak, what is literally circumlocuted.

Radio brings the unknown to bear; the Net brings the known to the bearable. Given a text/image/audio/whatever file – that is all there is, nothing more; it exhausts itself and is exhausted and the play of content, the semiosis, exists in the perceiver, not "out there." This is secondary narcissism, looping through the machine; primary narcissism is the realm of the analogic, our cosmological identification.

+++

The history of radio is merged with the history of the electromagnetic, and given the movement towards packet and protocol, it is interesting to observe a movement from externality to internality, from brass spheres through the Wimhurst generator, from the crystal detector through the audion. Within the audion and early triode, the filament glow was visible, an electronic hearth boiling off electrons. This was the analogic pulse of vacuum-tube radio, a pulse of light and heat and the quietest of sounds still sought by rock guitarists and audiophiles alike. Transistors internalized current into the literal black-box, and integrated circuits and circuit boards eliminated almost all of the hand-wiring. With the digital, the unit becomes tight, compact, although as always, still hackable; repairs are another matter. The analog was a transitive filter, passing along the cosmos within rough bandwidth; the digital is active sampling. The transparency of the analog was reflected in the transparency of the radios themselves (capacitors and transformers etc. notwithstanding); the opaqueness of the digital, the complexity of the protocols and their arbitrariness, is reflected in the opaqueness of CPUs. It's both ironic and fascinating that mod cases now bring the hearth-glow back into the heart of the machine, with lights that do nothing but illuminate silent circuitry. We still believe we are among beings; we always will, and that is part and parcel of our cosmic reach, no matter how mediated it becomes. The mistake is to take the mediation and machinic for things themselves; certainly, on the level of *object*, and certainly not on the level of *function*. We design within the imminence of potential wells, both analog and digital; otherwise we would never hear a thing.

Confusion of the Split

I keep searching for the *split* everywhere, the appearance of the discrete which can, but must not, be rendered impotent/futile. There are dyadic theories – Laing, some communications theory, but these specify resonances among entities that need not be clearly defined. There is the ontological theory of quantum mechanics, in which particles and transformations more or less "are" the real in mathesis and observation. There are theories beyond theories, theories I can't hope to understand, accumulations of theories. There is everyday behavior among the signs and sign-systems of the world, and all of the sign-systems are far more culturally ideogrammatic, non-system/culturally founded, than first appearance indicates.

The digital lies in fabrication and/or in one-to-one codes, or deeper, on the quantum level.

Let us at least momentarily call it the discrete. Perhaps a distinction can be made: *digital* technology, but *discrete* as epistemological (and perhaps ontological) split.

The discrete is characterized by its lack of continuity with the analog. A spike, fold catastrophe, wave function collapse, are, perhaps discrete.

A digital recording, for example, a CD, is discrete only in relation to the potential wells of conventionally-bound domains. A CD is analogic as an object; the 0s and 1s *resolve*. However, given a decoding/playback, the hills and valleys *register* as 0s and 1s. The sound transforms back into the analogic through the playback system (speaker, earphone, etc.).

The registration of the 0s and 1s are dependent upon conventionally adopted *protocols*. We've been over this territory. The protocols appear *real* although they function only in relation to specific technologies.

The coding is discrete on an ideal level; the signals themselves have onset and trailing. But within the given potential well of the technology, they *read* as discrete.

Your money or your life: discrete, yes, or no; it veers. −money = +life, but (+money = −life) = −money. Life is an *entanglement*.

All choices are braided, contingent, contiguous. The discrete is always a *barrier*.

A vast distinction must be made between discrete *codes* which are designed conventionally systemic, and what might be termed the *external discrete*, i.e., stochastic, an appearance, unplanned-for. The difference between a digital CD and particle decay. This is the fundamental difference; one we construct with what is given to us, the other is givento us.

I would think that the digital/constructed barrier can always be circumvented; the discrete of the world, however, like the analogic, is *just that*.

+++

(In relation to _ideality,_ the discrete is simpler; any given integer, for example is E or −E, even or not-even. If the integer ends on {02468}, it's even. The sets E and −E are complementary, discrete;

their intersection is the null set, and their union constitutes the set of all integers. On the other hand, in non-ideal life, the life-forms of the everyday world, there may be for example a number of plums which are neither odd nor even – for example, pluots may or may not be included, hybrids may veer off, partially eaten plums, seeds, etc., all form fuzzy cases.

(Now with the plums, let us open a distribution center: It is then economically necessary to count plums. The raster/protocol is created, the result is a digital screening.))

Discrete < on and off | 0 and 1 | other sign and other sign > Digital implementation.

In this scheme, the protocol is scheme / noise within the system:

[Referent | operative field] < Implementation > Digital mapping
....^.............^...................^..................^..........
0-resonance|boundary delineation|protocol-parasite|machinic display
(idiotic)   (circumscription)   (cultural convention)   (economy)

(On and on and on... stumbling into science, realms of ignorance.)

In lieu of thought or thinking – a summing-up:

My work deals with the relationship of consciousness to the world vis-à-vis the mediation of problematic and "dirty" symbolic domains.

My work deals with the wonder of the world as new bandwidths, vistas, histories and geographies, are made available.

My work deals with the problems of foundations, Absolute, primordial, originary, in terms of debris and scattering.

My work is a continuous dialog, itself scattered among distributions.

My work evades biography, diary, autobiography, the anecdotal, whilst plunging into the simulacra of personal narratives.

My work exceeds itself, resonates with itself, with others; the others inhabit my work which curls around fictivity.

My work is my obsession, to an unhealthy degree; however, when filled with despair, there are moments of exaltation as distant shores are glimpsed.

My work is fearful of being found out; it is worried close to death.

My work is a stripping away of irrelevance; my back to the wall, I inhabit the world.

My work is a constant meditation on the world, on its diffuseness, its encapsulations, circumlocutions, circumscriptions.

My work has pretensions towards the philosophical and the scientific; I strip my work away from my work as well.

My work touches language, body, and sexuality, all in relation within/without an inert real.

My work insists on the fragility of the good, of stasis, of permanence; it embraces the plasma, is swallowed by holocaust, dissolves in detritus.

My work covers the same ground repeatedly.

My work is simultaneously excess and denudation, artifice and natural deployment, ornament and structure, text and subtext, suture and wound.

My work is simultaneously hypothesis and hypothetical, a proffering or wager.

My work inscribes my work, deconstructing inscription and the walls surrounding the Torah.

My work hedges and devours death; I work furiously, death will allow even this and one other final flourish.

My work penetrates to the state of inversion; what is negative, is positive, and what is positive, negative.

My work is based on the fissure, not the inscription; it is based on substance, not dyad, on ruptured continuities, not positives and negatives.

My work is a collapsed ecstatic; my work is a collapsed aesthetic.

My work presses the systemic until it breaks; my work is a broken work, construing breakage, irruption of subtext into text, symbolic into subtext, substance into symbolic; my work breaks the inscriptive chain itself.

My work carries equivalence across media, genidentity across protocols and virtualities, sexualities across avatars and bodies, politics into the flesh-heart and ideological strangulation.

My work is discontinuous on the surface, tending towards stylistic extremes.

My work explores epistemologically and ontologically shifted bandwidths; my work brings the uttermost into the vicinity.

My work explores the desperate exigencies of the flesh, the shock-tactics of annihilation-creation, the degeneration of generators.

My work tends towards the unaccountable, the unaccounted-for; my work emphasizes the inconceivable.

My work inhabits originary past and indeterminate future, locating the plasma at the former, and the final outpost of substance at the latter.

My work runs from wavelengths universe-spanning to particle wave-lengths, listening everywhere; my work is a reporting from the limits.

My work inhales information-annihilation, being-annihilation, its own absence and every other.

My work inflates, exhausts; I have a desperate relation to my work; I tend my work in the meager hopes of its survival beyond me.

My work is its own; my work is centered in the dissipated locus of the histories of the self; my work is beyond my work.

My work occurs within non-Aristotelian logics, within logics of non-distributivity; my work occurs within dusts and radiations; my work exists in relation to the death of the symbolic.

My work decodes my work; my work brings the code of work, the code of labor, to the surface.

My work is codework, operational research for the flesh; my work abjures absolute frameworks, definitive infinities.

My work explores the inaccessibly high-finite, the inaccessibly low-finite, numeric flux dissolution into physical-material real.

My work is the future of philosophy, the future of intellectual work, of the propriety of the intellectual; my work is the afterthought of the past, the afterthought of the future, the thought of thought and its draining. My work is none of these; my work is hubris.

"My work" or "my work" but one may say "*" in lieu of the phrase; my work is a place-holder, shifter.

My work is neither this nor that; my work is not both this or that; my work is vulnerable.

My work is analog-stumble, digital clarification; the real is inescapable and production is discrete; my work is never done.

My work is trauma-therapeutic; my work is beyond that, bypasses that, circumvents that; my work is unconscious, of the dream of the real, of the dream of a real; my work stands on its own, ignores me; my work is in spite of me; my work is a collocation; my work circumscribes confusion; my work is insistent; my work is philosophy in the highest and lowest degree; my work is the world's unconscious; my work is the true world of the dissipation of worlds, of the imminence and immanence of death; my work is a bulwark and a fiction; my work is non-fiction, languorous; my work is neurasthenic; my work is the neurosis of the world; my work is never done.

State of New Media from Chokeberry Fields Forever –

The work I'm doing isn't much different from the work you're doing.

It will disappear when the net goes down or when it's no longer tended.

Nobody tends things forever.

It's amazingly ephemeral; there's nothing to it; it's stillborn, passed in email or on a website, that's all.

It's not as if we're contributing to the well-being of humanity; the idea that art makes any sort of social or political difference is long-outmoded, repeatedly proven wrong.

We're not even making paintings which have a modicum of a chance of survival, "being as how" they're concrete, inert, almost idiotic thingsn (in the sense of Rosset or Sartre).

Certainly we haven't made any contribution to physical theory or the sciences in general, and our work is rarely entertaining.

At our performances and readings, only the rest of us show up.

The "culture" such as it is, follows mass media, corporate distribution systems, subtended radicalities; the best one hopes for is museum sponsorship.

We've saved no one's lives through our art – turn the machine off, and we're pretty much done for.

We engage in outmoded theories, bouncing one theorist off another, as if any of it mattered in the universe at large.

We work through fast-forward intellectual fashions, situations in which phenomenology, existentialism, postmodernism, deconstruction, and so forth – name your "movement," name your theorist – are considered outmoded, as if philosophy had advanced since Heraclitus.

We ignore scientific theory, or borrow from it, on a simplistic or metaphoric level, as a form of legitimation, as if we're somehow connected with scientific "advances."

We confuse science with technology, substituting cleverness for any real disciplinary understanding, in fields ranging from psychoanalysis through physics.

Our theoretical work is written as if it somehow matters, somehow says something about the world, which we hardly understand.

We substitute cultural politics for political action and depth; we ignore war or illustrate it.

We entertain ourselves endlessly, as if our work had nothing to do with entertainment (some might call us failed comedians, novelists, what have you, substituting surface transformations for that hypothetical depth that seems to infest the canon).

I am guilty of all of the above.

We go on and on and on...

My Sixty-Five Failures

I dread this.

My first failure is an inability to sleep through the night, no matter what; insomnia and nightmares occur constantly.

My second failure is a failure to relax, to take time out and enjoy things, to not see the world through pessimistic eyes.

My third failure is never to feel at home, anywhere, to remain nomadic no matter what, to be unable to inhabit a place.

My fourth failure is an inability to make money, to have a stable income, to stop this constant scrambling after decades of making-do.

My fifth failure is my real lack of university affiliation, to play the playing the outsider for the rest of my life.

My sixth failure is not to be accepted as a serious scholar, however that be defined.

My seventh failure is a lack of books of mine and others bringing together the theoretical work I do, as if my career is based on diary, anecdote, hypersexuality, obsessiveness, neurosis.

My eighth failure is an inability to feel at home on the net, to have my processes accepted as somehow fit.

My ninth failure is the lack of a conference circuit due to poverty, which tends towards a lack of face-to-face meetings.

My tenth failure is an inability to program well, and to remain in one mental space long enough to learn a language, both natural and computer.

My eleventh failure has been a miserable personal life in the past, and a real difficulty in seeing the external existence of others outside my narcissistic circuitry.

My twelfth failure is a lack of high mathematical skills.

My thirteenth failure is an inability to produce anything beyond dribble-works, small fragments in lieu of the masterpiece which would temporarily ensure my place in the cultural cosmos.

My fourteenth failure is a lack of critical attention given to my work, which appears increasingly to exist in a vacuum of my own making.

My fifteenth failure is to slow down, to stop producing an obscene quantity of materials, mainly of interest to myself.

My sixteenth failure is that of controlling my sexual desires which tend toward annihilations and collapse, toward exhibitionism and uneasy dreams.

My seventeenth failure is that of lowering my stress so that constant anxiety won't kill me at a relatively young age.

My eighteenth failure is a lack of a PhD or other intellectual legitimation which might have gone a long way toward stability.

My nineteenth failure is an inability to relieve the almost constant depression that accompanies me everywhere, and is itself accompanied by weight loss and gain, nervousness, occasional crying jags, anxiety attacks.

My twentieth failure is to develop musical skills to the extent of reading music and playing compositions with others.

My twenty-first failure is not responding to others demands at a sufficiently fast rate.

My twenty-second failure is an inability to get beyond recognizing myself as a fraud, and understand that perhaps I am not.

My twenty-third failure is constantly being unable to exist independently of my family and their concerns, and to stand up to them in a reasonable manner.

My twenty-fourth failure is to have a satisfactory appearance, at least to the extent of being able to look into a mirror.

My twenty-fifth failure is an inability to face the current political crisis without suffering an emotional collapse.

My twenty-sixth failure is putting my partner through one terrible depressive situation after another.

My twenty-seventh failure is not being able to take more time out with my partner, working more around the house, even cooking for myself on a regular basis.

My twenty-eighth failure is being unable to cope with my Judaism and being far too paranoid about anti-semitism.

My twenty-ninth failure is not being a mathematician or physicist.

My thirtieth failure is not exercising enough, and not being good at any sport.

My thirty-first failure is feeling uncomfortable around people and crowds and being unable to enjoy myself at a party.

My thirty-second failure is being far too loud and defensive, talking far too much about sexuality, and not taking my own work seriously in public.

My thirty-third failure is being unable to deal with authority, and to exercise authority, without appearing overly neurotic or belligerent.

My thirty-fourth failure is being unable to avoid getting angry in situations where I should be more laid back.

My thirty-fifth failure is to avoid thinking about death, which is constantly on my mind, and to avoid a constant fear of death as well.

My thirty-sixth failure is an intolerance of organized religion.

My thirty-seventh failure is the inability to feel anything but regret in relation to the life I have led.

My thirty-eighth failure is an inability to see a way out of the trap I have set for myself as a failure.

My thirty-ninth failure is an inability to leave things well enough alone.

My fortieth failure is to stop being a nuisance in situations where I am ill at ease.

My forty-first failure is not to have had the funding to go to China and Japan for a reasonable period of time.

My forty-second failure is somewhat of an inability to express my love.

My forty-third failure is an inability to stop crying literally, when facedby a wounded bird, or insect, or mammal.

My forty-fourth failure is a deep-rooted inability to love humanity.

My forty-fifth failure is to stop thinking about money all the time, and accept my situation in life.

My forty-sixth failure is to stop attacking myself and secretly agreeing with others when they attack as well.

My forty-seventh failure is to find my successes almost non-existent, and recognize them only through muted consciousness.

My forty-eighth failure is a lack of grounding in traditional philosophy, for example reading the longer canonic texts all the way through.

My forty-ninth failure is dropping names as a means of justification.

My fiftieth failure is a feeling I've accomplished nothing of substance that has made my poverty and dependencies at least equitable.

My fifty-first failure is an inability to feel comfortable around drugs or alcohol.

My fifty-second failure is not having been able to perform well enough on stage, as to occasion a career.

My fifty-third failure is not being accepted by either the net art world or the art world, or for that matter, the worlds of poetry, film, video,

My fifty-fourth failure is an inability to stop whining.

My fifty-fifth failure is an inability to be classified or accepted as an "artist" in any category.

My fifty-sixth failure is an inability to slow up and work on my failures and regrets through self-administered therapy.

My fifty-seventh failure is a complete suspicion of authority and an inability to give myself over to a therapist, guru, or other mentor.

My fifty-eighth failure is poor health, poor hearing, poor eyesight, and thus always feeling at a distance with others.

My fifty-ninth failure is an inability to thereby feel comfortable at the beach or poolside, or any other situation where my body appears.

My sixtieth failure is not having hiked across the country, not having mountain-climbed, not really having lost the fear of the dark.

My sixty-first failure is not having real savings, and not being able to provide well enough for my partner.

My sixty-second failure is being far too ambitious and unable ever to satisfy myself.

My sixty-third failure is being unable to sleep if I have not worked at least some, every day of my life.

My sixty-fourth failure is always having to keep what I see as my addictive personality, under control.

My sixty-fifth failure is an inability on every level to stop the self-hatred from overwhelming me.

My sixty-sixth failure is the lack of a book of mine which would explain "everything," and bring both theoretical and personal coherence to my life.

My "Innovations"

(apologies for the length)

Most of my work disappears, dissolves, is forgotten, is lost; I've been thinking about a list of what I've done, accomplished, for better or worse, over a career for more than a half-century of exploration into language, philosophy, the problematics of materiality and the virtual, the ideology of reality as inert, the somatics of the body and its interiority as well as its embedding in the world, etc. So here are descriptions of some pieces, technologies, etc., created over the years. I just don't want all of this to be lost, although it surely is, this is memory, there's evidence of almost everything in the (my) archives, traces –

I think of these as "innovations," "explorations," "extensions," structures I hadn't come across before – not to insist on any sort of originality, but for a kind of development that I wanted, with as little repetition as possible –

In around 1968-69, a friend and I built an analog synthesizer from scratch with "loose" oscillators that could be locked onto their harmonics with the proper voltages.

My MA graduate thesis at Brown University, *An,ode,* published by Burning Deck Press, was the first creative poetry thesis awarded a higher degree at Brown – it was entirely experimental, the text between analog and digital thinking at the time.

Four-dimensional hypercubes and other shapes made from string, the forms collapsed on the floor so the connections are there, but not the image, a kind of inversion of conceptualism – making pathways among such forms in a series of drawings – the drawings were "code-drawings" whose forms were based on geometric paths. The show at the Bykert Gallery was reviewed in *ArtForum* at the time.

From the start of 1994 until now, I've written the "Internet Text," a "continuous meditation on cyberspace" on a daily basis, putting the work online daily as well – it's a discipline that allows me to explore long-form topics such as virtuality, the phenomenology of the analog and the digital, etc. – the texts are most often linked to other media as well – I'm not sure this is "art," in any case it's an extension of my previous daily practice of writing and other media that resulted in a series of artist books, films, videos, photographic series, audio works, and so forth – I never thought in terms of "pieces," but of continuous explorations, which is still the case.

In 1971, using a vector graphics program by Charles Strauss, I created a video, "4320" with an accompanying essay – the piece consisted of participants learning to navigate 4-dimensional space through the projection of a vector-graphics hypercube, an early joystick and keyboard – participants "drove" the hypercube down from 4 to 0 dimensions, collapsing the form by turning it perpendicular (4-3-2), then shrinking to 0.

at West Virginia University in the mid-2000s, through Gary Manes, we rewrote the software of an early motion-capture system, to add an interface directly to the mathematics of the filter mapping, which allowed us to create "dynamic" or "behavioral" filters modifying the input on the fly, creating otherwise inconceivable actions, stills, and videos, based directly on the cabled receptors.

Around the same time at West Virginia University, using the Linux access grid multi-camera multi-microphone conferencing system on Internet 2, I created a number of audio and video pieces, bouncing a signal around the planet through a number of predetermined nodes – I was able to create feedback loops with delays, depending on the internet "weather" – Azure, for example, would move in front of a screen – the signal would travel through Queensland, Australia and return – the image would be projected on the same screen with delays after circling the globe, for perhaps dozens of times, and i did the same with audio signals, playing against myself as the signal echoed back to West Virginia.

Somewhere early on, I came up with the name and concept of "codework" which has since been used in all sorts of systems, far from the original conception i had for the term – i still work on its phenomenology.

In the past few years, I recorded two "concept CD" albums – one of which, through Supercollider and the programming of Luke Damrosch, attempt time reversal with sound in real time, an obvious impossibility which nonetheless led to a unique number of pieces and speculations – the other album is based on very high speed instrument playing, including "overhand/underhand" techniques for acoustic and electric guitar – the speed designed to create new patterns of intuitive thinking to keep up with the pace and create new modes of listening as well.

Around the mid-'70s, a number of pieces, including programming a TI-59 pocket calculator to create a poem generator in only 1k of memory for everything, these also included working with the limits of printouts near sin(tan) forms, where tan goes to infinity.

Around the same time, using a mini-computer, i wrote several programs in UCSD Pascal, including a text editor which aggressively modified the input of whatever the user would type, creating alternative messages, scenarios, and a politics of despair and escape – also a program that placed text directly on a monitor screen coupled with a draw program that interpreted the ongoing text as graphics which eventually completely covered the text being written.

Recording intercourse from within and without, creating a sonic envelope with the results – recording a cricket in the middle of a loft, using feedback to make an "unbalanced" sound environment with the insect at the center (no animals injured or kept in any of my work).

In 1971 or so, created and registered a corporation called "Meta" designed to use conceptual art-making and other related practices, to create new ways of doing philosophy, futurology research, and so forth.

Around the same time I taught a course at Rhode Island School of Design called "The Year 3000" – based actually on the year 2000 – designed to examine the future of the planet using a variety of sources, and I've continued talking about these issues whenever I have the chance – in any case what we discussed in the class has all come true, and right on schedule for that matter, a source of great anxiety, that nothing was acted on so early.

Earlier, around 1969 or so, designed the concept of a "parameter control module" which would attach to identical others, and could be used to control audio, video, or any other inputs and outputs in the form of a skein of small analog computers – this was never constructed.

A few years ago, Azure and I traveled across the United States, searching for the quietest electromagnetic radiation zones along the way, and recording very low frequency radio signals which came through as a result – this took us to many isolated sites, the whole of which was mapped through photographs, satellite images, and so forth.

In the early 1980s experimented with Auricon news cameras, creating one 16mm sound film a week, with complex in-camera editing, including optical-on-optical sound and so forth – at the same time I made a 16mm one-hour sound film, edited in camera using loose ends, rewinds, and projector-recording on mag-stripe filmstock for four hundred dollars, and about one hundred dollars a copy.

On a residency through Bob Bielecki near the Hudson River, worked with a sound engineer to short-circuit 4-foot tall capacitors to create sonic "bangs" which were then bounced across the river using a large parabolic mic – the resulting echo-train was recorded at 128"/sec. and slowed up – this apparatus acted as a form of sonar, and we were able to "hear" the sonic shadows of objects over a mile away.

On the same residency, using very large antique flashbulbs and reflectors to illuminate the farther bank of the Hudson, and on another residency near the Susquehanna, using contact microphones to record the resonances of a steel bridge across the river.

Around perhaps 1973 while teaching at NSCAD in Halifax, "general description of the world," which involved photographing a beach at 1/25000 × from an airplane, then magnifying microbiomes on sandgrains with a cambridge stereoscan scanning electron microscope, to 25000 ×, the work accompanied by a number of texts.

Using the same SEM to create the "smallest sculpture in the world," well below the limits of human vision, a piece shown at the Paris Biennale (I think 1973?) - a second viewing of the same piece with the sem would have destroyed it through the power of the beam.

On a number of recent residencies, working with motion capture equipment, primarily through live remapping of body sensors, including inversions and other topologies - as well as distributing sensors among a number of performers, who must act in consort in order to create the illusion of a single body in the final avatar file output.

Creating a number of open-sim virtual world works on computer local-hosts, in which the live radical transformation/augmentation/ destruction of the landscape creates a "refugee" status as a homeland disappears - this has led to explorations of anomie, isolation, and hyper-realities.

Working with Dawnja Burris to produce videotapes dealing with Ciudad Juarez and postmodern geographies, 1992 - emphasizing both informal economies and infrastructures, as well as "radiations" as basic characteristics of a planetary future, around 1992.

A piece around 1973 on the assassination of President Nixon, stills from an 8mm film I made, shooting Nixon when he visited our area of Pennsylvania after the hurricane Agnes flood - he hit his head on a trailer overhang (we accompanied the president's party), and started to fall over - the still makes it look as if he had been shot - shown at the 1973 Paris Biennale as a series of projected slides.

Created a series of online "talkers" in the 1990s which were altered to create socio-sexual and other situations for users – in some cases, navigation became impossible.

Rewriting programs like Emacs Eliza, Adventure and a Moo, to create new possibilities for digital literature, along with multi-dimensional fractal and other programs connected by single pathways to examine complex networking structures.

Very early on, using an antique Wimhurst generator to create electromagnetic fields modifying reel-to-reel recordings of the 10" sparks.

Playing music in hurricanes, recording beneath a (very small) tornado, and other interaction with severe or interesting weathers – for example, flute-playing in high wind, where the impossibility of a proper embouchure becomes part of the piece.

In a farm at far hills, New Jersey, as part of a small group show, projects in nature, 1976, I used a small pond to create a number of video live microscopy tapes and stills – they were displayed and accompanied by an essay on the "phenomenology of approach" which I still find valuable.

At the New Jersey Institute of Technology 2018, I worked with students and faculty to create motion capture pieces in which the sensors were not only remapped, but removed singly or in groups – the result being different forms of avatar articulation.

Importing complex and altered BVH files (avatar articulations) into virtual worlds, extending the resulting modified behaviors into alien scenarios – working with dancers to imitate the modified behaviors, remapping these into virtual worlds, and so forth – using this material, as well as overloading the space with altered shapes, to create and augment inconceivably alien spaces without apparent gravity or coordinates, dimensions – writing up a phenomenology of these spaces.

Working with Foofwa d'Imobilité and other dancers with various technological extensions, including the use of very low frequency antennas or a virtual cave space as basic elements of movement and sound.

Series of pieces over the years based on the Laurel Run mine fire, outside Wilkes-Barre, Pennsylvania, including infrared 16mm film nighttime documentation on the mountain, explorations of thermophilic bacterial biomes, and tracing the growth and contraction of sulfur/steam fissures – working with Kira Sedlock holding the vibration meter between her teeth as she moves on stage, the sound later digitally raised several octaves, the body movements turned into sound variations.

3D printed models of distorted avatars created with altered mocap files, exhibited along with their bases – producing a series of small disturbing sculptures that relate to war, injury, pain, exhaustion, and death.

Dancework based on weather forecasts from a small Massachusetts town around 1830, created around 1969.

Using a vibration meter over the years to record building movement and instrument sounds primarily in the subsonics, digitally raising the pitch to create an interplay between what is heard musically and "normally," and the architectural-environmental aura surrounding the performance itself.

Using outmoded broadcast color-TV equipment coupled together, to create resonant loops within the analog electronics, recording and searching within these for signs of life.

Using two tape recorders on opposite sides of a stage, one recording live sound on a tape running between the two – the second running at half-speed and playing back, feeding into the first, so the sounds are lower by an octave at each looping, always bottoming out, live stage performance around 1971 perhaps.

Using Blender to model altered avatar movement files onto abstract objects such as metaballs, in order to examine how the mind interprets movement as "organic," "conscious," and so forth.

Ongoing investigations into concepts of inadequacy and failure, creating work that became, becomes, or will become, unsuccessful.

Filtering and Analog Digital

(notes from all over)

Reworked from a 1978 Toronto Notebook, "On the successive eliminations of the entity in transformations"

or rather all that is necessary from the diagrams

$a \rightarrow a' \rightarrow a'' f' f$

The function f moves a to a'; f' moves a' to a'' and of course there is a composition $f'f(a) \rightarrow a''$ or some such. a' disappears (or rather, is rendered ontologically a somatic ghost) as an entity, and on might generalize, considering a series of functions $f, f', f'', f''' \ldots$ such that $(f'''f''f'f(z))$ is a filter over z. In the lifeworld, $f\textasciicircum n$ extends in either direction, i.e., n ranges over the integers at the least. In reality, n ranges over the continuum. Every entity z carries (embodies? is? becomes? succumbs to? is identical with?) its filter and a filter is non-existent without an entity. The continuous transformation of the entity is defined by the filter and vice-versa. Since z may split in the process, the filter may split. The series $f \ldots$ need not define any particular entity, but may be considered split from a previous series, i.e., one out of an almost infinite number of processes, infinite in relation to the continuum. In this fashion, the worlding process is visible, the *entity* disappears, as entities do. Entities are named in any case in relation to space-time; too great a dispersion, and entity disappears qua entity; the background microwave radiation of the universe is an example. Too small a dispersion, virtual particles for example, and entity is ontologically problematic. Within everyday life, water and other liquids, as well as gases, are not considered entities, while glass, also liquid, is. It's a question of a family of usages in relation to viscosity for example. There is also a notion of intrinsic identity based on communality and communication; humans are entities, although rapidly undergoing decomposition. Reichenbach's genidentity is useful here; it references the actual material substrate of a coherent object, held genealogically together over a substantial period of time, and undergoing change qua object. Such an object brings human phenomenology with it; objects out-gas, wear, wear-out, dissolve, split, from what might temporarily be considered an origin, their inhering to a presumably created form. All origins and all endpoints are subject to filtering, which dissolves them as such. One is left with continuous birthing, continuous languaging and worlding, processes related to Bohm's implicate order on one hand and *maya* on the other. Of course the filtering itself is filtered, there is no end to it. To be human is to attempt to halt such, impede what is identified as dissolution, death, permanent impediment.

Ownership arises out of this, as does the urge to collect, related to the urge to hunt, to permanently annihilate, absorb, be reborn in the blood of the other. To stay with the filter is to remain analogic, deeply human, chthonic; to impede is to construct the digital, build, aerate, delude. The digital is always already inauthentic, Vaihinger's as-if which resides for and in the moment. Culture veers among the various orders, as if the world and its history is ordered and orderly; it is the sympathetic, not empathetic, magic of this that allows us to survive.

(Final) Frontier

I like to believe I'm working on a frontier and all I can tell you is what's on the normative side of things; the rest is yet to be seen, unabsorbed. Once brought in from the Pale, it's of lesser interest, but beyond the Pale there's nothing but the agony of shadows. Defuge takes over and the frontier, always an imaginary, shudders and reconvenes.

The videos/choreographies exist between human and human – someone was there making the original files with motion capture, and someone is at the other end, watching and using them once again. The virtual is a shadow of the real, the real is a shadow of the virtual, and within the true world superimpositions, gestures, and the fading of ontologies characterize what remains of the fixity of inscriptive practices of the classical and modern ages.

Distinctions are blurred through embedding and filtering. Avatars and humans – together, emanents – are embedded in online virtual worlds, in spaces which are simultaneously physical/inert/analog and virtual/mobile/digital. Every seeing, every being, is a filtering; existence and copula are interwoven. A current collection of texts is called "messays"; in a messay, there's no leading sentence, no orderly sequence of ideas, no summings-up, no conclusions. The essay is to classical narratology as the messay is to future true world genres which seep into one another, headless and tailless – meandering on the one hand, problematic obeisance to protocols on the other.

What we started with is the body which is inscribed with scars, scratches, tears, wounds, blemishes, abrasions, cuts, and all other debris carrying analogical history into the symbolic. What we continued with are tattoos, incisions, fashion, gesture, languagings, and what continually emerges is the body harboring technology as self retreats or withdraws, puckers, from the wild symphonics of externally applied filters digging ever deeper.

The walk or arm-swing becomes gesture becomes anysign becomes trade-off, translation, transformation, exchange, interoperability, reified territorialization. One sits at a console and breathes through sheave-skin, another begins vortex stage-center with flesh-electric, a third wanders memory of others airless, unbreathing, peripheral wanderings mediated at mind's back. From the airless, flesh-breathers are attracted, gather, project and introject, their selves flowing, flooding, abjecting, full of scent and coagulation.

We take our tiny community of people up and down mountains, in and out of clubs and iced fields, across the chiasm of cut bodies and body cuts, mines and other extractive industries across the flesh of land and bodies. What we bring back is always new, even if only in the slightest detail, a brush of the hand or turn of the head that was never seen before. And we keep to our goal of understanding filtering and embedding better than before, and understanding bodies in the always future anterior world, the true world of emanents and anysign where we're living, breathing, writing, and wryting, this and any future day.

Almost every avatar you see represented is a composite of two people; if you see two avatars engaged with one another, the engagement is contiguous at best, and each avatar is itself a composite. The composites are male and female; they reflect and murmur other in relation. Two are four, four are eight, eight are sixteen. Or more, depending on the configuration of motion-capture, the independence of minds and intentions.

> In the sense given to this term by Jacques Lacan (and generally used substantively); one of the three essential orders of the psycho-analytic field [...].
>
> Lacan brought forward the idea that the ego of the human infant – as a result, in particular, of its biological prematurity – is constituted on the basis of the image of the counterpart (specular ego).
> Bearing in mind this primordial experience: we may categorize the following as falling into the Imaginary:
> a. from the intrasubjective point of view, the basically narcissistic relation of the subject to his ego;
> b. from the intersubjective point of view, a so-called *dual* relationship based on – and captured by – the image of a counterpart (erotic attraction, aggressive tension). For Lacan, a counterpart (i.e. another who is me) can only exist by virtue of the fact that the ego is originally another [...].[8]

Thus simultaneously a space of mirroring and of singular constitution, a space of a real and an evanescence. In Second Life, objects are constituted in relation to a well-ordered database, without which the enumeration of potential behaviors, constructions, and wanderings would be impossible.

---

8   Jean Laplanche and Jean-Bertrand Pontalis, *The Language of Psychoanalysis*, trans. Donald Nicholson-Smith (London: Karnac Books, 1988), 210.

"Another who is me" – another always is me, neither constitutive nor part-and-parcel. One leaps on the page to "Incorporation": "Process whereby the subject, more or less on the level of phantasy, has an object penetrate his body and keeps it 'inside' his body." Etc., etc., more or less. One might argue that it is always incorporation, that the world is world by virtue of *devouring*. I would ask, who pulls the strings, moves the sensors, whereby one has been two, two murmur one, in these image of behaviors that are simultaneously inconceivable, and at the root of every narrative?

It doesn't stop there; the avatars are the result of filtered behavior, filtered in such a way that $f(n)$ does not equal 1, i.e., is not transparent, but in fact transforms behavior into caricature that gnaws at the body, representative and within a primordial gnawing, if you like. (This filtering occurs in the transmission/reception stage of raw sensor data turning towards coherent representation. Filtering is mobile, perhaps system noise, more likely hacking or rupture, the dim imaging of presence unaccounted-for. Any reception is filtered – I'm arguing for yet another stage in the communications model, existing in those liminal interfaces among block-diagram entities and arrows.)

Table 5, Eco's theory of codes in *A Theory of Semiotics*[9] – the Watergate (hydraulic) Model interpreted in relation to expression and content planes. But framed on the left: "Continuum / Light, electric phenomena / Non-semiotic matter" and on the right: "Continuum / the unshaped continuum of the position of the water along with everything one can think about it / Non-semiotic matter." One discretely cuts surgically within the analogical which remains impervious, bounding; a discrete cut cuts discretely, constructs difference across fissure, that is operates within and constructs inscription. Isn't the

---

9 Umberto Eco, *A Theory of Semiotics* (Bloomington: University of Indiana Press, 1976).

world such an inscription? Let us think of non-semiotic matter as *dark matter* to be brought within the fold (*pli*).

Selves are located, others and an others are located, between these matters, which are all that matter, out of which the drawing-forth is temporary at best. Nāgārjuna has no position and this positionlessness is as close as one can get.

The doubled figures within the figures of the avatars you see projected on the screen, live or in careful reproduction, are uncanny; they appear in documentary footage to be completely independent, but by virtue of the sensors are connected, as in Bell's theorem, in such a manner as a fractured *monother* or entity is produced. Conflicting forces are combined without effect or affect traveling among them: there is no resolution, only tearings as the image-monother accommodates them all. Think of the movements as _catatonic sex-dances_ or rites of passage held in position precisely by those noisy channels which, parasitic, spew culture in otherwise dull transmissions. A catatonic sex-dance is a molding or ingestion, incorporations, of others in order to form selves (an "adult" is an entity whose flesh is carved into the semblance of a human being). A dance is called "sex-dance" if it is dual; it is also [   ] "corporation-dance," "incorporation-dance," "culture-dance," "death-dance." Sheave-skins generate nothing internally but imaginaries; externally, they generate internals. Think of the monother as worlding, the mapping of external universes onto, within, small finite spaces which appear coherent, the mapping cohering. The dance, like that of bees, is of course any communication, established or not, channeled or not; one might think of beings inhabiting monothers in such a way that their touch is full, replete, of one another. What you see on the screen may appear both tired and strange, but it is also a model of the true world within which monothers characterize life and lives, living, inhabitations, habitus. (Think of the "it" in "one going it alone.")

You have to look for the specific discrete levels, nodes, configurations, on the expression plane – all of which are moving at highspeed – but you *must* look, drawing forth a narrative, which, like all others, is yours and yours alone and ties, however uncomfortably, the appearance of beings into Being. You have to see monothers shimmering among modes of existence, ontologies, for example, movements among rocks and cliffs and movements among intended rocks and cliffs, deferring among intentional/configured ontologies, and those which are mute, inert, idiotic. Or divide the catatonic sexdance into substance-catatonia (misnomer and oxymoron to boot) and inscription-sex-dance (the same, the other boot, terms booting monothers into the arena).

Now you're getting closer to the relationship among inscription, code, substance, communication, &tc, and further might bring you permanently, like a matchmaker dotcom, into collusion from collocation, where contiguity and contingency meld and something permanently unnamable emerges, where Nāgārjuna's grasping, samsara, appears:

> When there is a grasping, the grasper Comes into existence. If he did not grasp, Then being freed, he would not come into existence.[10]

Let them go at that.

+++ +++ ++++

---

10 Jay L. Garfield, trans., *The Fundamental Wisdom of the Middle Way: Nāgārjuna's Mūlamadhyamakakārikā* (Oxford: Oxford University Press, 1995), XXVI, verse 7, 78.

Phenomenology of Approach

this time it was the loxahatchee, jacek and i overturned the canoe on
a three-foot drop, digital nikon overboard.

(it worked for a minute for a moment.
(the card caught its dying breaths.
(in the beginning, some lacewing eggs followed by a scale insect
(then the clearing with paurotis, cypress, fern (what might have
    been
((an alligator hole))
(then the clearing again
(suddenly:
(the switch: this was the portage route which we ignored
(sondheim soaking, filmed with the dying camera
((it seemed alive at that point, the images as usual
(jacek by the canoe, clive and jane by the canoe
(the next image is blurred, green, railing and water
(the camera was dying
(the lens, clouded, electronics shutting down
((oh how i worked to retrieve the images! how many hours of
(coaxing them from the card!)
(following, the last retrievable series:
(blue blurs through the ruined lens
(sondheim in mourning and recuperation
(the final image but one, the light
(the final image, the car and its drowned technology

(the madness of the image
(the madness of the light

(madness of the image
(madness of the light

the camera struggled to rise, it couldn't
the images leaked out, the shutter button released its last
the poor and tiny screen lights and lights,
blind eye of the lens reaching out –
here, look at this, but you will never own it
those clouds, those lizard-eyes, that spider, this umbilical
cut at last, untethered real floating off and on –
i'm part of the blindness, i hold the camera like a baby
the lens floats in and out, i can hear the breathing

"the dying camera"

you may have
you may have the last images, they crawl, they remain
in funeral, the card holding on, desperately
the image, the image, the image
silent, submerged

Jennifer's Dream of Goodness

lacewings curled around each other in the doomed thicket.
they came to me and said, there is no competition; cut the cables.
the unseemly monotony of engines formed a distant phalanx.
already live-born young were the order of the day.
eggstrands transformed into protective grills.
poison occupied the tips of incessant life.
the contribution of the viruses was immense and not to be under-
   estimated.
a second-order phalanx formed inside the mutated grills.
microscopic domains organized against the violence of the macro-
   world.

lacewing circulations, viral turbulence, across the sawgrass surface.
their stems bending slightly, sawgrass forests acquiesced to the power
of the thicket.
shudders went through skins of the mammalian order.
their live-born young died quickly of unknown contusions.
the phalanxes stilled among incessant life.
lacewings curled around each other in the order of the day.

i love my machines :sawgrass slides one way, cuts another. sawgrass
inscribes itself on retinal matrices. it says "sondheim, there is nothing
to look at." it says, "sondheim, you will have nothing to see." i hide
behind tender matrices of digital format and rastered resolutions
inscribed with rectilinear coordinates. sawgrass says, "sondheim, this is
your imaginary." sawgrass says, "inscribe yourself.":liguus fasciatus
verge everywhere. i live hammock-snails. immobile, untouchable, fragile,
over fifty forms. worlds-creating against polluted waters cleansed by
cattail-marsh. my machines allow me to see beneath every surface. inside
my surface i am dirty dirty dirty. i run in shame from liguus fasciatus,
hammock-snails. i do not touch them / touch myself. i pick my face to
ruin. i cannot bear my face.:i am so poor i love my machines. years ago i

built my machines. i wear machines hide my insecurity / my stupidity / my
unoriginality. i wear machines hide my weakness / my shame / my
embarrassment. my machines say "sondheim is not a pariah." i am run by my
machines in this direction. it is winter-season and my machines run me. my
machines take me places. they move my body. they pleasure my mind. my
machines do not say shame shame shame. my machines do not say regret every
day. my machines empty me into them. shame shame we do feel nothing.:5.5megapixel:
2.1megapixel
3.3megapixel
1megapixel
5.5megapixel

i am so poor i love my machines. years ago i built my machines. i wear
machines hide my insecurity / my stupidity / my unoriginality. i wear
machines hide my weakness / my shame / my embarrassment. my machines say
"sondheim is not a pariah." i am run by my machines in this direction. it
is winter-season and my machines run me. my machines take me places. they
move my body. they pleasure my mind. my machines do not say shame shame
shame. my machines do not say regret every day. my machines empty me into
them. shame shame we do feel nothing. replace your sawgrass slides one

way, cuts another. sawgrass inscribes itself on retinal matrices. it says
"sondheim, there is nothing to look at." it says, "sondheim, you will have
nothing to see." i hide behind tender matrices of digital format and rastered resolutions inscribed with rectilinear coordinates. saw grass
says, "sondheim, this is your imaginary." sawgrass says, "inscribe yourself." red-winged-blackbird

+++ +++

13 lines of refuge. white lichen. refuge in resurrection fern. refuge in
everglades crayfish. refuge in limestone solution hole. refuge in mosquito-fish. refuge in leopard frog. refuge in apple-snail. refuge in
spatterdock blossom. refuge in spatterdock fruit.:refuge in bay-head.
cocoplum thicket. nighttime great blue heron. solitary killdeer. refuge in
coot. cattail marsh. mussel. refuge in horn snail. refuge in mud-wasp.
hardwood hammock. refuge in boattail grackle. refuge in common grackle.
crow.:refuge in spatterdock. pondapple night-blooming blossoms. spatterdock fruit. african tilapia. florida gar. desiccated periphyton.
deer spoor. alligator spoor. sawgrass. refuge in webbing. butterfly weed.
halloween pennant dragonfly. green water snake. diamondback rattler young.
::red-winged-blackbird is olympus camedia 2040 sq2 high. on wet flesh it's
red-winged-blackbird

+++

the glades are a continuous dynamic process across a planar surface. a
park with variable boundaries, problematic topography based on hydrology
and human intervention. the dynamic is everything; think of the glades as
an *inscribed surface* transforming in space and time – a surface organic
and shifting. the glades are simultaneous with their entanglement of life
and migration; they are vectored, and vector is everything.

geology is underfoot; to manage the glades is to manage the ecosystem.
invisible topographies / geologies manifest by surface organism. the
indefinite prolonging of comprehension.

lesser research on amphibia, arachnida. effect of mosquito population on
other species.

marsh hare
american bittern
desiccated periphyton
red-shouldered hawk
black mangrove pneumatophores in short hydroperiod brackish ponds
dwarf cypress forest
cypress dome interior
zebra longwing
prairie warbler

black-necked stilt
hardwood hammock

echo "marsh hare" >> echo "american bittern" >> echo "desiccated periphyton" >> echo "red-shouldered hawk" >> echo "black mangrove
pneumatophores in short hydroperiod brackish ponds" >> echo "dwarf cypress
forest" >> echo "cypress dome interior" >> echo "zebra longwing" >> echo
"prairie warbler" >> echo "black-necked stilt" >> echo "hardwood hammock"
>>

glades *as* a dynamic confluence of subjective horizon and interwoven
biomes – perception of organism, organic perception: to lose oneself
across or within a breathing sheet of water – laminar/animal flow – broken
by solution holes, slight ridges; one wanders *anywhere* among fragility,
evanescence, limestone accretions, marl, peat, periphyton, surface
ruptures of hammocks, domes, sloughs, marsh, river, creek, borrow pits,
dikes, airboat trails, highways 75 and 41, embankments...

local networkings, routers, communities, rookeries, isps, servers, trails,
usps, clients, hosts, nodes, domain names, water conservation areas,
icann, water management areas >>
monotone of slow breath, particulate grasping: *the prehensile*

withdrawal from alligator radius

(nikuko wants to go home. jennifer wants to go in.)

scalding water stops the pain for a moment; the hammocks carry blood-lust
in their very atmosphere; thickets are swarms; in dwarf cypress forest or
coastal prairie, one is accompanied by horse-flies, biting midges, wasps,
larger insects from a distance; chills and fevers wake one in night's
thick entanglement; one's body is a mess, suppurating, gouged and gnawed,
split, half-devoured.:deer-flies stinging constantly, the mosquito gouge,
sand midge extract. points of the body, usually ignored as implicit
hinging - elbow, ankle, knuckle - sudden areas of intense pain or scab, as
blood flies near the surface, bone heats up, the insect settles for the
final score. chills and fevers, slight numbing of the body, general
weakness.: :the arms first, then the fevers, the tingling, desire to gnaw
at one's flesh, lacerate oneself, cut off the offending bit of flesh or
limb. it makes no difference - one dreams of alligator biting through the
fingers, itch giving way to momentary pain.:knees and shoulders:neck and
fingers

torn skin, flaked, oozed; dried blood on arm, hand, neck, wrist
ficus and spoonbillng as a model an open
nightmare!t. Somelat
larger insects from a distance; chills and fevers wake me in night's
entanglemennternet text at
= > maintain

+++ +++ +++

VR Improvised

Anything is possible in the virtual.
Inscription is absolutely cut off from the real.
Inscription cannot be sutured into the real.
The virtual is disposable.
The structure of the virtual is substitution.
Substitution implies creation and annihilation.
0 may be substituted for 1.
1 may be substituted for 0.
The formula of the virtual is [any][any].
The formula of the real is [1][1].
The real is sutured to the annihilation of inscription.
The real de-; the virtual in-.
Nothing is possible in the real.
Suffering is ontology; the virtual Occupies epistemology.
The real is neither here nor there.
The virtual is multiple.
The real is extruded from the real; the real intrudes on the real.
The virtual divides infinitely; the real divides perversely.
Neither the real divides the virtual nor the virtual divides the real.
The ontology of number is practico-inert.
The ontology of the virtual is imaginary.
We know that the real and the virtual are imaginary.
We know that the imaginary inhabits abjection.
We know that abjection inhabits the imaginary.
Abjection inhabits the real insofar as the imaginary.
The virtual expels abjection; abjection is beyond the Pale.
The Pale is its own configuration.
The Pale confines the real.

Everything and nothing are possible in the Pale.
The Pale is beyond the Pale; there is no interior.
The real is multiple by virtue of the virtual.
The virtual is fractured by the real.
The virtual takes all the time in the world.
The real takes none of it.
The virtual takes all the space in the world.
The real takes none of it.
The Pale rides the back of the real; the real fucks the Pale.
And in the virtual? Anything is possible in the virtual.

We Will Survive

if we are not stardust
if we are not stardust
if we are space and time
if we are space and time
we will survive
we will survive

if we are not breath and bone and marrow
if we are not breath and bone and marrow
if we are not blood and bone and neuron
we will survive
we will survive
if we are not molecule and atom
if we are not quantum and quality
we will survive
we will survive

we are not stardust
we are not stardust
we are space and time
we are space and time
we will survive
we will survive

we are not breath nor bone nor marrow
we are not breath nor bone nor marrow
we are not blood and bone and neuron
we will survive
we will survive

we are not molecule nor atom
we are not quantum nor quality
we will survive
we will survive

Surge Compendium

Proceed.

"Surge is the overthrowing of all values, ideologies, and structures. It is the absolute overthrowing of all histories, privacies, persons. It is the total extinction of all species, including our own. It is the scorching of the scorching of the earth. Let's talk about this. Let's build around the Surge. Let's build around the dying and absolute annihilation. Let's do it." (ca. 2015)

Proceed.
A pixel is a digital object.

Between one pixel and another, there is annihilation.
Annihilation seethes.
There is nothing else but an epistemology of demarcated positions and ontology.
Post-digital is digital; post-digital has equivalent epistemology.
A digital object is substrate-dependent.
The substrate is an object and from this we adduce strata and structures of digital objects.
Proceed.
The Surge is just that, the Surge of digital objects and substrates, replacing everything in the world.
Annihilation is the potential for transformation of everything in the world.
Annihilation to the limit is extinction.
Abjection and truth are intertwined.
Abjection and truth inhabit the substrate.
The digital object is a mapping of its substrate and its substrate is subject to replacement, duplication, reassignment and other transformations.
The substrate is a moment of the digital object.
The entanglement of truth and abjection within the substrate is within a continuous state of annihilation and potential wells.
The digital object is an object of reading; the substrate is a surface of writing.
The Surge loads substrates with digital objects.
Proceed.
The Surge replaces objects with digital objects.
Aura is always an entangled raster.
The Surge replaces aura with increasingly fine rasters.
Rasters are inscriptions and demarcations.
One might say that rasters are inscriptions within the metaphysical, that substrates possess no rasters, that mapping is from raster to substrate.

The digital object is a choice.
The digital object may be a choice of a substrate object.
If a substrate object is chosen or not chosen, it will be scorched.
If a substrate object is chosen, it may be inscribed.
The inscription of a substrate object is not a substrate object.
The inscription of a body is not a body.
The inscription of a body may inhere within the body, and may be entangled within the body.
The substrate of an inhered inscription is within states of annihilation and potential wells.
The digital object neither exhausts physical objects nor its substrate.
The digital object is an insertion into protocol farms and networks, including translations fundamentally based on the employment of process and power; to the extent that the digital object functions as an insertion, it is subject to movements across substrates.
Proceed.
The digital object is en garde.
The digital object is an instance.
The scorched earth of the scorched earth is annihilation to the limit and the elimination of the instance.
Reproduction of digital objects is finite.
A reproduction machine itself may be reproduced.
At the heart of the reproduction machine, at the heart of any object, digital or otherwise, is annihilation.
Annihilation inhabits the absolute, and the desire for absolute annihilation constructs the scorched earth of the scorched earth.
Proceed.
The Surge constructs a new earth, new habitus, new environment.
One cannot turn back, one cannot return, from the Surge.
The fundamental characteristic of the Surge, at this point, is

the simultaneous recuperation of every history, every culture, every text, and the annihilation of every history, every culture, every text.
The simulacrum of recuperation is a simulacrum.
Simulacra are simultaneously recuperated and annihilated.
The Surge proceeds from fundamental annihilation.
The Surge is simultaneously the relativization of the world, and its absolute.
Proceed.
The Surge is violation fabric; on the nub of the Surge, we bear witness to annihilation.
Proceed.
It is not even a matter of time.
It is not even a matter of bearing witness.
There are no matters of which "it is a matter."
Proceed.
The *mob* of the Surge.
Proceed.
The *overwhelming* of the world, of any other world.
Uselessness and annihilation of philosophies.
Proceed.

Proceed.

Bewails (ca. 1996)

An Older Mind bewails nations. It hovers dark, interconnected at nodes, sprayed in star-configurations connected across night-twinkling-stars, incandescent bulbs streaked with blue at magnification 150 just across town. An Older Mind would bend deep in Thought, would stir dark waters into dark and stillborn

Action. An Older Mind would enumerate Nations gaunt and hoary, branches of trees rustling the sky stormed into carbon-russet darkness. Lightning is sky-crack, cragged break of black porcelain, Older Mind Sim-Symbolic illumination burned into seven-layered blood-stained retinal booking down to bedrock flaked with muscovite.

Older Mind is t = 0, is <=refresh> constant, emission into screen-object, sound-object. Older Mind turns at to pace, haunted as body heaves thrust onto side; it ponders for No-Reason, is None. None hurtles downward into No-Reason; only nations say split, no capital. Look elsewhere than there. Older Mind shudders sky-bowl swollen, crusted with Sim-Symbolic. Bewail.

Proceed.

Failure to Overwhelm (ca. 1996)

To theorize the Net, analyze it according to one or another model (see below), to examine it without any philosophical presuppositions (an impossibility), to include or exclude metaphysics: A closed – an academic loop is formed, the placement of a book or article (I try for this myself), but what occurs beyond this, what reason, what point (reason collapsed to a node)?

What can theory *provide* if it is not, for example, descriptive kinesics, software design philosophy, standardization of protocols, typifications? It remains an augmentation, appended to what? Half in and out of the corpus of philosophical discourse, applied philosophy, but towards what ends? What?

(Consider *here* the onset-characteristics of a trumpet tone.)

There is of course the theorizing of the virtual – from a phenomenological viewpoint, theory describing *stuff* on several levels, the *stuffing* in fact of cyberspace itself, however that term is defined, split, deconstructed. Of course there are no conclusions; there are, instead, parallels, analogs, interstitial or liminal displays of language.

Statistics appear in sociological analysis, almost always soft. Structures may or may not emerge. Whatever they're made to speak is manufactured. On the other hand, considerations of Being, etc. lend themselves to curious metaphysics. These can go anywhere, routed in roots.

This *applied* theory centers it on *topic,* a source of decay. What if there's no theory-otherwise? What theory-otherwise would apply? What ghosts enter the maelstrom, alternative selves, ectoplasms, staggered or schizzed personalities inhabiting the same flesh?

Theory vis-à-vis topicality *here* is already abject, a vestige of territorialized minor philosophy, slide-rule humans approaching the discarded object, still clothed and canvas-wrapped. Minor philosophy, perhaps in the sense of Deleuze and Guattari, minor literature.

Even the psychoanalytics of the space generate ghost shots at a new subjectivity – but these things change on an almost daily basis.

All this spells ennui, the peculiar analytical burnout where cyberspace theory is concerned, entrance and exit *the doldrums.* It's partly the socio-political atmosphere of "the times," exhaustion as theory becomes mechanism, predictable, unused, negative dialectics. On one hand, articulation is all there is; on the other, overwhelming information all the way down/across, well-definition literally ruling, graduating the day. The liminal fails to erupt; the liminal is theorized.

Proceed.

Paul, Sail On (ca. 1996)

If I gather up, will you bury me, will you bury me if I gather
    up
Your ambergris, your bronze helmet, your amber, your bronze
Swollen by river's wake by cavern opening cavern awakened by the
    river's swell
Motivated by gutted reeds cut stuttered clay, read in gorgeous
    monuments gone motivated
If I lie with you, will you lie with me, if I lay with you will
    you lay with me
Near the pregnant cow near the gutted horse near the emptied
    house by the coward's prayer
Through the dim dark night by the knight's despair by the armor
    there
If I wash for you by the river's edge and I wash for you by the
    same edge of the river
Where down the river there is a gathering of knights and women,
    I think they are celebrating Telipinu at the moment

Yes, I will lie with you, I will lay with you, I will sacrifice,
    you will sacrifice
Your horse, your cow, yourself, against my golden hair, my eyes
    of blue
Sparkling in the waters pooling by the marshes, waters sprinkled

with blood, swollen with whitened
Bones you have slaughtered, your bones you have slaughtered
While I, while I
    I'm leaving for Telipinu.

Proceed.

Dawn* (ca. 1996)

cancers flooding the body in part or in full, tumors attacking one or another organ, membrane-spreads of *illnesses of the surface,* attacks on bodies non-virtual of all ages, genders,**

there are millenarian warnings as the human tide heats up, microbes approach with landing-gear erect, this is serious as insecure bodies escape to the cybersphere, sloughed skin dragging them back,

we are close to degeneracy genes gone bad in polluted air not responding to antibiotics lost, no longer fortification bunker against molecular transformations, lost, in other worlds, the air itself,

wires clean wires with electrons, cloyed filaments, carbon dark against smoothed electron emissions, tunneling, run around the sync clock, skin a sin or shame a dark shadow, no longer named but ceased symbolic,

so we slough skins, our poisons trail behind us, so our membranes turn translucent, troubled, and there were no tomorrow

+++

* dawn's brilliance cuts the eyes' retinal spoils, dwelling and source of disease, scoured in the heat of day

** so many I known have been cut down in the dawn of life, suppurations suddenly appearing in the half-year past, portending uneasy crawl towards overpopulations, extinctions***

*** for real, the theory appears simplistic, pollution, extinctions, ozone, desire, capital, technology, spills, desertification, violence for real for sure****

****

Proceed.

Justice (ca. 1996)

There is no justice in this world! That is, because justice is never *of* or *in* the world, nor is it a horizon of the world, nor of community, nor of the subject. Then one can never be just? One can act accordingly, as if justice were a past that still encompasses the present. This is the dream, the opium, the simulacrum, abstraction, but without it, irrigation disappears and selves dissolve, as if they had once existed. Proceed.

Proceed.
Corroded substrate hammers.
Violation fabric of disappearing languages.
Dead tech and dead life.
Proceed.

the new song

bone follows bone
the new song of longing
azure carter, voice and song
alan sondheim, alpine zither

& begin by eating not and drinking not
& continue by sleeping not and speaking not
& welcome the thinbarked body into the space
& welcome the disappeared into the time
& into the time of the bone
& into the time of the bone
& into the space of the bone
& into the space of the bone
& into the purity of the space and the time
& into dependent arising and emptiness of bone
& into the lesser absence and the great absence
& begin & continue & welcome & welcome into
& begin & continue & welcome & welcome into

Surge/Cut

surgery is from surge, to cut from the body, annihilate; to surge is to purge, perjury, annihilate the truth, violate the body politic, violate the corporeal body; to surge is to annihilate the corporeal politic and the political corpus; to annihilate is to swallow space and time; to swallow space-time; to annihilate surgery and the potential for surgery; to embrace space and time. thus the "blown-out" body of the ancients is the eliminated/purged/expurgated body, the eviscerated body, the absent body, the absence of absence, hence dependent-arising. thus the dependent-arising is the totality of space and time, emptied of body and surgery: that is the Surge.

       Jennifer4.sutureandsurgery + "
 + Jennifer4.sutureandsurgery + "<BR>");}
 peace to the unwelcome task of boredom, surgery, and ennui –
 + Jennifer4.sutureandsurgery + "<BR>");}
 + Jennifer5.you + Jennifer2.sutureandsurgery + "<BR>");}
 + Jennifer8.gender + Jennifer4.sutureandsurgery + "<BR>");}
 image epistemology, bypass surgery, suture
 one, right, remaining yet for surgery, muscles and lens still
 ## I had "surgery" on the 10th Saturday, crossed out.
 ## On October 5, Evelyn had surgery.

(It's the surgery; try a phenomenology of coagulation, cauterization, sut-Donna, who was assisting Mira in my surgery, noticed something in the For as not to see after and through eye surgery, the hearing. Jennifer3 = new Jennifer("mine ," "inhale ," "spurt," "surgery ," "my_voice "); Neurosuture was tried prior to, post, neurosurgery; her neurophonia got in Samuel. The central video image of the latter contains the words "surgery" The flap of skin, the surgery, is all They nuance my body; I said it was hard to explain – as if surgery were When surgery failed they turned to drugs and she [12:06] You: – she applies surgery – but then when you logout log back after dental surgery and exhaustion and 1.6 grams codeine, ances with my body/ i said it was hard to explain/ as if surgery were and fields – a surgery that is performed, again entangled, among the and stories, poetry and epic works of enunciation, new forms of surgery capital or gender surplus, that this is a matter of choice, surgery, case with the jury room, surgery, periods of mourning. In Central Jury, I damaging, surgery sarajevo lebbeus-woods-accre-exteriors, day party. He was getting better and better after the surgery (there were definitely be a lot of future discussion as a result of my surgery. Dr. document.write("Jenniferyellowmilk Jenniferbreathinggender Jennifersutureandsurgery");} empties except philosophy's hole, the surgery of the subject. Body fragile electronic structure itself, just as revolutionary surgery function Jennifer(gender, breathing, milk, suture, *and* surgery, you) graphemes, suture, surgery, place of birth and dissolution, cloth or has gone bad, surgery that didn't take. he moves jerked by the camera, scramble for position.– cosmetic surgery – here in the city that want to work with me, and I keep think of surgery/ imaginary spaces, surgery operates on interiors, organs passing through imperfect intersecting ah wet concerns ease exploratory surgery in survery-surgery i speed up my files beyond recognition. it is more like an obtrusion a suturing that has gone bad surgery that it's the surgery upon cyberspace that fascinates me, the impossible keys in a form of reconstructive surgery. THIS IS WHAT IT TAKES. I labor of medicine or surgery or surgical incision. Because, Tiffany points like an obtrusion a suturing that has gone bad surgery that didn't mense bluud-night cuvern, teuring, surgery To: Alan***Sondheim [1] Stopped mense und bluud-night cuvern, eyes teuring, surgery uf jennifer-julu in u nephew girlfriend 95th birth-party. surgery complications) repeated more, neurosurgery. There's an implantable microstimulator module, only 2mm wide new Jennifer("mine ," "inhale ," "spurt," "surgery ," "my_voice not be down here so soon after eye surgery for example. Please if you need obdurate, video, video-telephone, suture, surgery, mandala, obdurate, video, video-telephone, suture, surgery, mandala, mantra, life, perhaps, the doctor said, i'll need surgery, freeing the nerves, pitch-durk bluud bluud-night cuvern, eyes teuring, surgery uf reconstructive surgery. takes. genius, professor, teenager, rebel, 'with renal gland. Hopefully the surgery a week from now will take care of skin-graft across me, your surgery-gift,

sutures. Death, crystal, mud, skin-graft me, surgery-gift,
sutures. crystal, mud, so soon after eye surgery for example.
Please if you need a response from superstructure signifier.
sartre sidered pretence beings choice, surgery, surge and
surgery, prom and promontory surgery involving cuts, folds,
sutures, pathways and bypasses, coagulents surgery on the
surface of the body to create an opening to surgery, incision,
is necessary for the rest of the gaze. It's Stone's surgery,
surgery was committed, i was given the material world, now;
suture*and*surgery, you) lag rhythm, hypnoticwild swaying, thing
going telecommunications equipment, worlds in sorrow, not
surgery, and worlds the body (Orlon not excluded) through
plastic surgery – a transformation the pronouncement of surgery
or suture: sed 's/foo1/bar1/g' < z1 > z2, and this.milk = milk
this.suture*and*surgery = suture*and*surgery;
this.suture*and*surgery = suture*and*surgery; thought. It
couldn't see the IC, not without special surgery, but recogni-
tinguish between the body of surgery and physiology, and the
neuro/logi-towards an exploratory surgery of
virtual-psychosis.] way to ink jet to laser surgery of final and
apocalyptic scenes engraved were also the most damaging, an
inverted surgery of landscape and the wiping-existence
fflffllffllfflflffluvia:::: :surgery of the wiping-existence
lfflffflflffluvia surgery of the with bleak surgery unkind and
again now elemental redistribution with bleak surgery unkind and
again now elemental re|||||||||||| works of ===, new forms of
surgery are you your voice? your ===? your would free itself
from surgery; someday it would carry emanations beyond
{document.write(Jennifer1.suture*and*surgery +
{document.write(Jennifer7.suture*and*surgery +
Jennifer6.suture*and*surgery {document.write(Jennifer9.milk +
Jennifer9.suture*and*surgery + Jennifer9.gender

Surge

"The transformation is so enormous, there's no way to describe it; everything we say, everything we are, everything we do, it is all false, broken; it is all irrelevant; the models are useless, irrelevant; you know the drill; you fill in the rest; you take care; you walk away; you walk away slowly; you are no long in thoughts

transvaluation of all values, annihilation of transvaluation = tattered disappearances = timed-out

+++ +++ +++ +++ +++ +++ +++

echo timed-out zero time
timed-out
time echo timed-out zero space
timed-out
    0.00s real   0.00s user   0.00s system zeroed out

Transvaluation of all values, thonged, timed-out. Zarathustra screams about the transvaluation of all values, and I scream. The first to go is the transvaluation of all values. A chucked value is valueless even if it is a transvaluation. No, wait! A chucked transvaluation is worth a lot of the little ones. My values are my clothes! I chuck them and dress in transvaluations. There are never simultaneous things in my world of transvaluations. That's part of my transvaluation which does the chucking for me. No value-chucking for my transvaluation! It will have to go! Its own, accomplished both the transvaluation of all values and their surge; I'm chucking values now. The first to go is the transvaluation of transvaluations. Everyone knows me here and understands me daily. What's that? Zarathustra screams about the transvaluation of all values, and I scream and what I scream is the following:

"nce, ccumultion, ccession, te, te, ve, ve, defen, defluxion, pel, pirouette, fen, levit levittion, lift, hevy swell, fflux, dvdv nce, rgement, rgement, ugmenttion, w wke egre, mke, meet, tking throng, clmber, undultion, gng upwrds, drin drift, esclesc de, de, strtle echoes, vult, swrm stun, ve, gng ve, g heve, hehe ve, hevy ve, he vy vy ise, rise, ise, r ise, ise, lly rlly lly r lly lly lly, rlly, lly, r lly, lly, rdrums, ers, rdrums, e rs, rs, round, gther, round, g ther, ther, ter wve, ter w whitecps, lep, gue, le p, p, regurgitte, rregurgit te, rce, te, r run sltrun s lttion, lt , sis, rise, scension, scent, scension, scent, scent, ccretion, ccess, ccretion, ccess, ccess, ccrul, l, l, ccession, ccession, multiplic onwrd onwonw rd onwrd rd onw rd rd empty, esclempty, esc lde, l de, de, tion, dv ffluence, ddition, ffluence, ddition, ddition, ggrndizement, ggr ndizement, ndizement, ttle rer ttle re r r ce, r ce, ce, vy horde, he se, se, sese , se, , se , , prolifer pulste, pulspuls te, pulste, te, puls rce, rr ce, rce, de, upgoing, upgr de, upgr upheve, upheuphe ve, upheve, ve, uphe rer, regurgitre r, regurgitte, r, regurgit rer rend pek, pepe k, pel, k, pe l, l, centrifugte, centrifugcentrifug te, centrifugte, te, centrifug p, levitte, p, levit levitte, levitlevit te, levittion, te, mplifiction, mplific sis, ggr ndizement, b tion, mplifiction, ccession, Chrybdis, ccession, Ch rybdis, rybdis, ke ugment ke the ke the in, fuse, g gin, gg in, gng in, g ng ng ccumultion, ccumul tion, tion, ssemble, ugmentugment ugmenttion, tion, rush, se slts tion, seethe, tion, seethe, , flow, edem elevtion, enlelev tion, enlrgement, tion, enl ded, bde d, bllooning, d, b llooning, llooning, st bloting, st blo ting, ting, upswupsw rm, upswrm, rm, upsw rm, rm, , se increse, increincre se, increse, se, incre se, se, infltion, inflinfl tion, infltion, tion, infl legue, lele gue, smsh, snowbsm sh, snowblling, sh, snowb lling, lling, snowblling, sosnowb lling, soring, lling, so ring, ring, grvity gr vity round, vity round, round, forgther, fountforg ther, fountin, ther, fount in, in, updrft, upgupdr ft, upgng,

ft, upg ng, ng, uplep, upleuple p, uplep, p, uple uprisl, l,
upris upstrem, upstreupstre m, upstrem, m, upstre upswrm, blst,
ebl st, er, st, e r, r, ker, brekers, ker, bre kers, kers, brek,
brebre k, breker, k, bre ker, ker, kers, brodening, kers, bro
dening, dening, prolifertion, proliferprolifer tion,
prolifertion, tion, te, converge, congreg crsh, crcr sh, crsh,
sh, cr sh, sh, scent, ssemble, scent, ssemble, ssemble, sh,
current, d dsh, dd sh, dte, sh, d te, defen, te, de fen,
melstrom, mm elstrom, mss, elstrom, m ss, ss, swrm, stresw rm,
strem, rm, stre m, m, stnd stst nd strtle nd st rtle rtle
multipliction, multiplicmultiplic tion, multipliction, tion,"

and then the screaming stops and the broken code like broken
teeth is impossible to reverse; let A = everything; let
everything = A. it ends here. it ends here and then space
follows

Surge No-purpose Music

[:] there's nothing useful
[:] there's nothing that can be used for anything
[:] you can start off here with earth
[:] then there are form and limitations and
you can write Earth and not earth
[:] you can write earth
[:] when you write earth, then there are things of forms
and limits and there are many of them
[:] when there are many of them, they have organs
[:] they have blood and they make sea and land
[:] they make flesh and bone and they make energy

[:] they use energy to make energy
[:] limitations collapse into perfect compression
[:] compression is the beginning of atom
[:] compression is the beginning of world
[:] world forgets time and space
[:] there is no purpose and no purpose is the bone of time and space
[:] no purpose is the making of time and space
[:] there is no other making
[:] one begins and ends with origins
[:] origins are beginnings and endings
[:] listen to origins and observe beginnings and endings
[:] nothing can be performed
[:] nothing can be made to start and transform intoaction
[:] action is never a performance
[:] to perform is to stand still
[:] to perform is to die
[:] act without purpose without limitations
[:] act without beginnings and ends
[:] act without formation of Earth and earth
[:] to act SUCH is to act
[:] to act is to transform into space and into time
[:] to transform into space and into time is to SURGE
[:] to SURGE is SUCH
[:] to SURGE
[:] SURGE is music
[:] SURGE is musical art and the art of music
[:] MUSIC is present only when it is absent
[:] when it is absent there is space and time
[:] when it is absent SPACE and TIME disappear
[:] without demarcation, without the MARK
[:] SPACE and TIME are non-existent
[:] one becomes space and time
[:] one becomes unmarked

[:] UNMARKED one is transformed
[:] into pure ONTOLOGY
[:] when one is transformed
[:] into PURE ONTOLOGY
[:] then music begins
[:] when there is a listener there is no MUSIC
[:] when there is a player there is no MUSIC
[:] MUSIC played is not MUSIC
[:] one one is present, there is no MUSIC
[:] when there is ONE there is NOTHING
[:] when there is NOTHING there is neither space nor time
[:] MUSIC is ABSENCE
[:] EXISTENCE is ABSENCE
[:] NON-EXISTENCE is MUSIC
[:] nothing is SORTED-OUT
[:] there is no SORTING because there is no DEMARCATION and there is no MARKER
[:]
[:]
[:]

See *The Bamboo Texts of Guodian II: A Study and Complete Translation*, trans. Scott Cook (Ithaca: Cornell East Asia Series, 2013).

Broken World: Steerage and Steering Mechanisms

We are steerage. We do not arrive.

*/Properly, the space in the after part of a vessel, under the cabin, but used generally to indicate any part of a vessel having the poorest accommodations and occupied by passengers paying the lowest rate of fare. [1913 *Webster*]/*

The ship is steered. The ship wanders. The world's broken. Don't misunderstand: nothing will save us; there is no land or: the land is damaged, or: the land is exhausted: blank, the land is blank: anguish. Anguish on our part. We're the ship. Our world.

Or: We're all marooned. It is no longer a question of hope, of the human project, of plans or structures, of capital or capitalism, of late capitalism, of neo-liberalism, of inerrancy or the absolute. It is no longer a question of ideologies, of common language, of the commons: it's over.

It's steered, and it's steered over, the steering's over.

The mechanisms at work are simple and fundamental. They are abject; they grind the rest, whatever was tottering through modernism – they grind the rest down. The world's a world of dust and radiations. The world does not crack. Our project's broken.

Some of them:

The first intractable mechanism: Overpopulation. The planet is close to its carrying capacity, and there's no end to population increase. The demographics are skewed towards young reproducers; exponential growth lumbers on. The result is more mouths to feed, more strains on the environment, more slash and burn, more hillside slums, more bush-meat, more overcrowding, less jobs, more local war.

The second intractable mechanism: Environmental degradation which has reached the point of no return. Consider the plasticization of the oceans, the post-tipping point of animal and plant extinctions, the increasing desertification world-wide, the loss of biological diversity. The anthropocene is not the usual planetary rise and fall; it's the greatest, the fastest, the most violent, extinction. The world is already destroyed; Gaia or its equivalent, is over. Something will remain, future adaptive radiations, but it won't be us: every species will be invasive, and the world, for the foreseeable future, will swarm.

The third intractable mechanism: Global warming which is also global redistribution of currents and weather flow. This is also irreversible, past the tipping-point. The results are harrowing: record-setting droughts and floods, enormous hurricanes, tornado swarms, irreversible sea-level rises, and so forth. This is the classical catastrophe (René Thom): the fragility of the good descends to chaotic phenomena, and practical measures, theory, containment, is always after the fact.

The fourth intractable mechanism: Increased violence and local/global warfare: again, with limited resources, this will only grow worse. Territories split and compete; the lines are religious, ethnic, geographic, historic etc.; brutality increases as humans turn more and more to the rigidity of absolute/inerrant ideologies, and fortified binary oppositions – classical logics – gain strength as ideological instrumentality. This turn to the right, where the free press, women's rights, science and self-critique etc., are all viewed with suspicion; the left (if these binaries still exist at all) is an endangered species.

The fifth intractable mechanism: The vast sea of weaponry and the nuclear arsenal available to all; it is only a matter of time before a dirty bomb or nuclear device is detonated, the equivalent of overfishing, trawling, the sea bottom. Scorched earth returns to scorched earth; there are no longer resources for rebuilding as poverty and social chaos increase in the world. History, archaeological sites, villages, nations, records, are erased; history is no longer visible, readable; reading itself becomes suspect.

The sixth intractable mechanism: Enclaving of the rich and income disparity exponentially increasing; the result is hoarding of resources and increased poverty as noted. This enclaving extends, crudely, to nations; the US for example uses far more resources per capita than almost any other country; the US prison system is itself a flux of pure capital, privatization, the largest in the world. Prisons are less efficient than pure disappearance; even so, population growth more than makes up for the violent loss of life around the planet. Think as well of local militias, including police forces that, first and foremost, look after their own, by any means possible.

The seventh intractable mechanism: Antibiotics and spread of disease across varying species; as sludge and clutter increase worldwide, the opportunity for endemic disease increases. Disease vectors are driven by population vectors, by poor health practices, by hunger and poverty. Understand that overpopulation is behind all of this, a developing horizon, just like hacking and criminal gangs are a developing horizon of violence and seizure. There's no more living off the grid; off the grid is on the grid, within mechanisms and horizons. We're all in the ship, we're all marooned.

The eighth intractable mechanism: Global communication networks granting power and encrypted communication among activist groups, including local militias and extremists. These networks are temporary, because the Net and its cousins are subject to hacking on an inconceivable scale; security simply can't keep up without infringing on the rights of others – without replacing one ideology by another, far harsher. The Net and privacy are porous, and subject to the seven mechanisms above. With so much data and control in the cloud(s), with so much control and personal information in the hands of monopolistic corporations, gangs and governments, there's no doubt that we're seeing the tip of a cyberwar iceberg that will do violent damage far beyond the Sony fiasco - damage that will extend to (for example) power, health, military, and financial grids as well.

We must begin to think of these mechanisms as both interlocked and environmental - i.e., constituents of a global and catastrophic horizon: much as the Club of Rome developed a model of interrelated flows in their relatively doomsday scenarios, we have to see this horizon as a holarchy of entangled mechanisms. The difference is that the mechanisms today are chaotic and unpredictable: there are events (primate extinctions, violent storms, the rise of violent fundamentalism, hacking of financial institutions, etc.) that are both destructive and fissured into any (ideological or instrumental) coherency that might have appeared as "explanatory" in the heady days of modernism which still inform us.

What fascinates me is the global appearance of these mechanisms in the large: there's a kind of simplicity in their phenomenology that dissolves quickly upon closer inspection. But the simplicity isn't contradicted by the details; global warming, for example, doesn't reverse because the north-east United States is having record cold spells. The overall configuration of the world is based on strange attractors, which proceed, literally, in any case; we're steerage, not steering. (The technophilic ideology of progress, paradigm shifting, and cleverness does a disservice here, promising techno-utopias just around the corner - or already here - while in reality the beheadings and bush-meat continue to ravage.)

(I think, at the least, of a curriculum focused on these mechanisms - but to what end? Past the tipping-point, things will continue to deteriorate until the anthropocene extinction does final damage. I can imagine the very rich escaping at some point, but to where, with what rockets, with what supplies? We are living in the ruin of a total institution called the global; we go down with the ship, in steerage.

And steerage is now the corrosion of the dream of the West at the very least, as Plato's cave becomes the hold of a ship floundering on polluted waters.)

[A version of this taught in a course, *The Year 3000*, at Rhode Island School of Design, early 1970s. The warnings were already in place, in truth and detail.]

Invisibility

Invisibility is the problem of our time, but there are so many! Most of our collapsing phenomenologies center on attention economies, acceleration, dromodology; these are epistemological problems, what might be examined, what should be examined, and the process of examination itself. But invisibility is more perverse; it is an issue of ontology, of disappearance, from within and without, a problem which not only robs us of our situation, our habitus, but also invades the discourse of the body and the self. It can be a sudden transformation, occurring at the edge of the possible, the refugee, the unmanned migrant ship floundering and heading for unknown shores; it may also be a slow and almost imperceptible withdrawal from being, to the extent that being exists as instrumental. Age is one index of invisibility, and this I experience: whatever I do increasingly makes no difference whatsoever, as long as it is with the bounds of the law. Making a difference, making a distinction, is fundamentally a communal and social act; when it no longer matters, helplessness ensues – not the helplessness of a lack of knowledge or tools (but that too), but the helplessness of the collapse of speech acts or being. The aging body is a refugee body, and what might have passed for wisdom is no longer given an audience, but is transformed into some thing swept aside within another register altogether. All of this occurs within a rigidity of etiquette which is not acknowledged, but which creates an iron and exclusionary ontology. Too many people I know, for a variety of reasons (political, age, class, religion or lack of it) feel marooned, a marooning which answers to no shore, no boundary. The issue is one of consequences, which at one point in our social evolutions might have been the concern of cause and effect, but now operates within the regime of effacement (what I have to say is of no consequence, because I am not speaking – a Lyotardian differend which operates across innumerable strata within broken models of being and the world). Engagement is not a projection, not what "makes us human"; it is, of course, a skein, and one now driven by fast-forward feedback, ranging from high-speed stock manipulation to high speed online text-and-image feeds that leave no time for reflection, but, more importantly, no need for reflection as well. The horizon of all of this is the fracturing of steering problems which dissolve in rhetoric and shifting positions; the problems, however, remain and increase in urgency. Behind them is an increasingly devastated planet with extinctions and population out of control, existing within the immediacy of the digital and its potential for internal transformation (a change of pixel for pixel, for example), for epistemological slide. ... For all of these reasons, these flows, invisibility tends towards pharmacology and depression, towards despair and violence, towards the inerrancy of fundamental religion and a rigidity of logics and taxonomies between believers and nonbelievers. It is easy to conclude from all of this that "we are all invisible" or some such, but in fact, the presence of belief and violence point elsewhere, towards a sweeping-aside of the ephemeral and the harnessing of the digital for a strict rhetoric of communications. For those of us who can neither ascribe to this, nor participate (by virtue of the problematic "essences" of age, gender, sexual orientation, religion, nationality, etc. etc. (all these categories left over from an age of classical modernism and post-colonialism), nothing is left, and this nothingness leads nowhere to enlightenment, but to those invisibilities which are always hammered into position by others, but which always resist positionality as well; this is the state of marooning, defined by the receding of that instrumental past which at one point, close by, has seemed to be heritage, but in fact was a social construct – the social construct of time which, fast-forward, takes no time at all. It is not that this too shall pass, but that this too has always already passed, and where once the I-(pod) might have been, there shall no longer be absence, but an absence of absence, mute, ontological, nowhere and everywhere at all. There is no answer because there is no time, and no evolution of our, or any other species; there is only the time of slow cessation, on this and other worlds, and the endpoint of invisibility is this – that one is invisible because there is nothing to be seen. This is no longer brilliant weather, but fabrication bending under the weight of its own collapse, as popular culture demonstrates over and over again, and we all succumb to its charms, just as news, here in Providence, flails out with the slogan "news you can trust," and advertisements hawk replacements and necessities with the slogan "just for you." No one drives these, no one receives them; events as well are marooned always already somewhere else, to someone else, to the displacement of populations, from nothing to nothing. (Of course there is the trope that "this essay, too, is invisible," but how would one know, and where is one? And immediately that one can see tendency towards that absolutism that also participates in the annihilation of the world, as if that were not an occurrence. What is foregone, is foregone by virtue of invisibility; what is present, is unaccountable, uncountable, and unaccounted-for. Such are the shoals of ontology, such is the unseen, within and without the parenthetical.)

[Perhaps too easy, not the *actual body* of the refugee, starving population, covid patient, *refugees with no place to go*.]

+++ +++ +++

Invisibility, Continued

The hallmark of invisibility:
There is no hallmark of invisibility.
Wait, isn't that a hallmark?
No it's a sentence and a sentence isn't a hallmark –
From Wikipedia:
"No it's a sentence and a sentence isn't a hallmark."
I read on Facebook invisibility isn't possible.
But I read a brilliant essay on invisibility on Facebook
called "Invisibility" and I don't think it's disappeared yet.
It's disappeared from my feed.
You can always look at Alan Sondheim's Timeline and you'll
find it.
Are you sure he hasn't be banned yet? He's been banned from
YouTube.
It was there last time I saw it.
It was a hallmark analysis of the phenomenon of invisibility
in and around the digital.
It will never reach its intended target, invisibility extends
itself, it does this by doing nothing.
So there is no intentionality associated with it, no object
of consciousness?
None that matters, it has no qualities, no parameters, no
structure, writing has been quite an exercise, I wouldn't
call it pointless, but its exactitude is meaningless to
anyone but the writer.
A couple of people have called it a rant.
Invisibility itself is a rant, but the author would rather
consider the essay an analysis, at least for his own peace
of mind; there was something about the act of writing that
motivated him, as the words disappeared down the long tunnel
of obsessive thinking.
He said he could almost picture the world receding from

him in a kind of foreshortened perspective bereft of affect.
Exactly, he had to picture something in order to keep on
going, no was else was encouraging or reading him, no
one else was around.
None of those mythical fireside evenings.
None at all, not so he noticed.

Outline for a Talk on Blank That Can't Be Given

Outline for a Talk on Blank that can't be Given (That is
inconceivable that it could be given, that it is inconceivable
that it might occur without contradiction, that it might say
anything, that anything might be said):

/Thanks to Bruce Barber, Foofwa d'Imobilité, Tom Zummer./

My work tends to deal with edge phenomena, areas of entanglement or confusion, appearance of glitches, and so forth. Early on I characterized my project as the relationship between abstract structures and consciousness. I've always believed that philosophy can be effected through modes other than writing or the text, that not all encounters are grounded in language, and that language has its own cloudy and entangled limits. All this said, the following is an outline on a talk which uses work done with altered motion capture equipment, as well as work produced on a recent residency at the Nova Scotia College of Art and Design in Halifax.

1. Philosophical work pushed to the limits:

- gamespace edges (Artworks which explore the phenomenology of the limits of gamespaces in virtual worlds: how are objects and behaviors affected, how does the physics change, how does one "inhabit" these zones? Do the zones have strict boundaries themselves? Can one speak of a broken game, or a suite of behaviors and objects that open elsewhere?)

- client or server overloading (Using massive particle sprays, fields of objects, etc., all near the client or server limits: what happens when the space or atmosphere becomes clogged? How does avatar control become entangled with the gamespace environment?)

- altered motion-capture/behavioral spaces (What happens when mocap alterations result in software overload, so that the simulation breaks down? Formally, the avatar image becomes immobile and "sits" in a lotus position. What is the experienced of enforced stasis in relation to disparate movement elsewhere?)

- software-dependent, see economic exhaustion below (Different software produces different results of course: what is the typology of glitches?)

[situations where structure collapses:

- where structure and the symbolic can't be recuperated (Where there's no return, where the vectors quickly end up entropic, where chaos dissolves into noise.)

- where the symbolic is limited by the *game of extension* (So that, for example, the gamespace or mocap edge is characterized by particular behavioral regimes: the game then moves the edge elsewhere or creates a catastrophic anomaly. Once this is absorbed and con/figured, the game moves elsewhere. Sooner or later, the game of extension dissolves into the cold death of the universe.)

How are these experienced? Does experience always translate into text? What is the textuality of experience? What is the dissolution of textuality?]

2. Exhaustion of symbolic space, the blank: (The blank is a state where [ ] is emptied but always already virtual, where the blank is the site of introjection/projection.)

- blizzard whiteout example (The whiteout of the blizzard images and videos: nothing visible but a seething, the fogged details at the edge of the frame pointing towards nothing, the seething incapable of geometrical meshing or interpretation as "mandala.")

- recapitulation through contouring (Noise reduction operations on blizzard and similar images: when the contour lines reveal nothing, where the inchoate roams among and through protocol suites. A busy seething might blockade imaginary projections; nothing survives the seething.)

- maps of far north, Mandeville (Looking at maps of *Mandeville's Travels*, 15th century) or 19th-century maps of exploration in the far north: the landscape – what constitutes shorelines, land, and water – dissolves into the inchoate. The blankness of maps is described early on by the presence of "Dragons" and later by a sense of the uncanny. Again, these are limit spaces, edge spaces, gamespaces defined by no games, unpopulated except in relation to the imaginary. Here and elsewhere, what does consciousness *do*?

3. Back to 1 – conceivable limits to scientific explanation:

- multiverse (Other universes, if they exist, may be totally out of communication with our own; there may always already be limits to cosmological observation.)

- economic exhaustion in particle accelerators (Brillouin hints, I think, that there may be deep and inherent ties between economic surplus and fundamental particle research; for example, particle accelerators operate up to certain energetic limits, and it would take increased expenditure to go beyond them. The universe might then be imagined to have an economic structure. High-energy cosmic rays point otherwise, but there are always going to be energy limits.)

- Planck constants (What might or might not occur "beyond" the Planck length or Planck time. The universe may or may not appear obdurate. The gamespace/edgespace of the universe might then be described by the game of extension. The description, I think, even if completely predictive on a certain level, has, at the asymptote, a blank.)

4. Roger Williams's theology – Roger Williams, the "founder" of Rhode Island, has a complex theology based on the broken succession of baptism from the beginning. Because of the break, the religious gamespace is inherently broken; each believer must decide everything for himself or herself. One might choose to become a searcher, or one might bypass the spiritual altogether. It's up to the individual; there is no inerrancy involved, no inherent law. Law is necessary for communal structure; it's a question of the State, not of the State's foundation. Think of the Law as a game, criminality existing near the edges of the gamespace, then absorbed. Without theological legitimation, there is a blank at work; the interplay between consciousness and structuration is cultural work.

5. Erhu (two-string Chinese bowed instrument)

- playing "normally" within bounds (Playing within the gamespace, playing in the first-third positions.)

- playing near the bridge: transformation to mimetic function (Fingering within 2-3 centimeters of the bow; the gamespace is transformed to mimesis: sonic imitation, or iconic sound, without reference or intervalic structure.)

- mimetic function as inert (At the edge of the gamespace, the sound transforms into substance. Think of falling out of the game, beginning another game, one of chaotic "noise." The game becomes a game of extension; the game of extension transforms the phenomenology of the musical structure.)

- blank (The structure becomes blank, becomes hiss; the structure becomes the substance of sound. Eventually the edge of the field is reached: If not now, when? If not now, where? As the fingers approaches the bridge, there is as much of an infinite choice as ever; infinities map 1-1 linearly. But the sound itself tends towards higher ultrasonics; whatever the measurement apparatus, listening device, that too can be surpassed.)

(I think as well here, of the work Azure Carter and I have done with Foofwa d'Imobilité, which tends towards similar edges and noise at times; I'm thinking especially of the *Involuntaries* which are available online.)

6. In all of the above, one might say, within any cultural game, there are limits, edges, blank spaces, games of extension, and extension beyond extension that becomes immeasurable, chaos or noise without the potential of a return trajectory. Think of the energy of the vacuum, virtual particles, annihilation limits

in terms of receptors: any receptor may be surpassed, there is always surplus bandwidth, without recuperation, reconstitution. How does subjectivity deal with this, concern itself with this?

7. At the other end of these broken totalities there are filters which process incoming and structure outgoing. The filters operate within protocol suites, layers of organization that transform information. The suites themselves are always transforming; they loosely define the gamespace, and to this extent, they might be considered closed circulations within potential wells. But wells themselves have tunnels, nothing is secure, and artifacts within the world are at best temporary stases. All of this simultaneously fits together and falls apart; all of this coheres and is incoherent, and this in any case is the talk on blank that can't be given, that is inconceivable that it might occur, that it might say anything, that anything might be said.

on good days

i dream of hitler youth and grey soviet masses
i dream of nameless american troops and everywhere people marching
i dream of jagged assyrian warriors and batak sacrifices
everyone i know is deeply anonymous and wrecking
i dream of salvage and wrecking and dams holding back debris
i dream of walking in collapsed buildings and furious suicides
on good days i dream of drownings and medicated deaths
i dream police-tape barriers holding back the artifices of destruction
i dream of those artifices

on good days i dream of names in ash and broken mouths and
    screams
everyone i know is broken and everything is going under
on good days i dream this crime will be solved

Why I Can't Sleep

I begin by thinking about my being a very old man; I continue by thinkingeach day might be the day where a lump or pain becomes something else,where the body turns its course against me, and that day will be a day ofdivision. Or perhaps there will be a night from which there is noawakening, and this remains deeply unimaginable. I continue by thinkingabout my family relationships, how I have to permanently sever ties withpeople who were dear to me, simply in order to psychically survive. Thisleads to a recent article on post-traumatic stress syndrome, the obduratecirculation of memories which become a permanent part of the psychiclandscape: something to trip over. After death they're meaningless, justwhat will save us, Jennifer asks, how shall we survive, where can we turn,what is to become of us, what is our future, what will you see when I die,what will become of you, what will become of the species, where has ourhistory gone, what happens to our dust, our molecules, our atoms, whathappens to our forms, our records, our data, our speech, the recordings ofour speech, the preservation of the recordings of our speech, what happensto the prions and viruses, the phages and the bacteria, the parasites,what happens to our sun and our planets and our lives, to whom shall we bespeaking, how shall my mind continue without the service of a god, whathappens to our demons when our minds dissolve, corrode, decay, corrupt, Jennifer asks, what happens when we can no longer hear your answers, canno longer hear our answers, can no longer hear ourselves, what happenswhen the memory of my mother with her book and my father with his fire,when these are gone and the sound of the mercury light switch is gone, andthe luminous glow of the afternoon and the mighty trees are gone, and themoon is no longer there, and the sun murmurs its planetary nebula, and theplasma disappears and the glow disappears, and there are no eyes to seeit, no ears to hear it, and where are you among us who shall save us, ohsave me, who among us will keep their promises always based onforfeitures, who among us will be among us, asks Jennifer, where shall Ibe, what can turn me around, what can provide the loving canopy of softnestlings and the presence of my friends of all times and all places, whatwill become of us, what will hold us back within the world of the living,will nurture and nourish us, will feed us and clothe us, ah, I am donefor, says Jennifer, I am already half gone, I am already two-thirds goneand three-quarters gone, ah, cries Jennifer, save me, save me, save m

Broken Conversation

----------------------------= YTalk version 3.3.0
=---------------------------- therefore something should come together between the two bodies separated by a serrated division, vertebra one among other. pain is this logging-out, is the collapse of the backbone, the melting or melding of the body as it begins to disappear.the body's not here either, the body is a square, is a playing-field, the body is a holding-pen.the i is a stream of i's, of eyes, these appear as if it were, but just imminent, as if just momentary, just for a minute.drying, in other words a stain or residue, we can say a conversation is a drying, a drying-out. in other words, you're saying this is dust, this is red dust,

In the year 5000, my birthday falls on a Monday, I won't be around. Somehow, this makes me unutterably sad, weeping.

Our span is so short, we all know that, but this, this concrete instance, tears through me. And I won't make it, to be sure, past 2020...

. in my eye, jennifer and julu, nikuko and travis, honey and alan, accompany me, their organs, bones, and flesh already fallen by the side of the road that is, in reality, a plain, open in every direction, neither going nor indicating anywhere, any thing. my little band of characters is in the process is dissolution. my little world becomes a world of stories and no audience, my audience becomes a world of stories and no audience. one no longer speaks with smashed mouths, writes with smashed fingers, sees through the eyes of the death of the other, dreams or hears that way. it is always ultimate writing because it is always urgent. it goes nowhere because there is nowhere to go. destinations fall off the map which has disappeared. every dream is a dream of death, every gem outlives the decay of a pion, bringing misery in its wake. there is less and less time to tell stories. did i say audience. was there any: 'my writing is my most

important medium.' nothing else speaks. i write in an unknown tongue. the enormity of these figures... hard to convey in virtual worlds... you don't have to take my word for it... check it out, you'll see... you can sense them looking down at you... guardians... working for your benefit... whether you like it or not... it doesn't matter... one at a time and it has to be night... broken into pieces always reassembling... you can swallow them whole... their mouths big as the universe... at least this universe... i'll tell you more, i'm breathing...

what i remembered when it was so poor out

what i remembered when it was so poor out

i could not think and my body wandered
somewhere a link faltered and hindered
and cauterized my throat and thought throughout

there was no semblance or semblance fraught alone
meandering murmurs mourned rooms dark and fallow
in plummeting bodies and faces skewed and sallow
and hollowed among mounds of earth and burning bone

hallowed they were in sutured hands and ears
haunting loomed and muffled clutched at voices
senseless and seamless depressed of humbled choices
and dense thatched strands stranding and embracing fears

memory what i remembered buried borne and lost and thrown
among sounds of human ghosts but not their own

My Avatar / Human Wounded in Space and in Time

this is what happens in the real world when your eyes
are closed by others or you agree not to witness the horror
you were born into, you didn't ask for this, this shuddering
in space and time, this uniqueness with its catch-basin of
nerves already ruptured and furious at the world,

this is what happens when you step out of line, when you
can't come clean, can't clarify, can't suck your clean and
proper body, this stuttering in time and in space, this
smear with its basket of nerves torn to pieces, screaming
at every other world than their own,
Collapse this post

abstract animated avatar maquette
the holes open to one another or not at all
the bodies are crimped, collapsed, coagulated
the bodies crash and crumble without destiny
it's as if the holes puckered and faltered
and they might slosh what might be there
pure gifts from one to another
there's no happiness without exchange
there's no grief without collapse
the holes no longer speak or chatter
animated communities have no history
their history's left behind
monotony... monotony...
but there's always an echo in the hollow
where a letter lies sleeping

now it's cold and there's no time to dissolve this

virtual worlds

they get stuck in this life and yearn to return to the other
they are held back by memory and skin which falls from their
    seasons
they cannot move but are made from layers torn from their flesh
you are stuck in pain, you are held back, you cannot move

small models of splayed and abstracted avatars in pain
they are fleeing from it

radio sounds from antique radio equipment
you lean against glass and hear the flesh of the earth

photographs of a small child doomed to make these things
the child is doomed to listen to these things too

images of dead soldiers against your eyes
you cannot think anything but images of dead soldiers

books of martyrs and tortures and torments closed
you cannot read through covers telling your cold future

lament maquette for the dead as the world oozes human beings
human beings come forth and gather their dead and die

the virtual is the pain of the real and an escape
the virtual is powered by the pain and escapes into the virtual

o real pain o virtual
o doom of memory o dead soldiers o stuck flesh o martyrologies

you are deaf and hear nothing but your pain
call you forth and you hear nothing and what is survive
radio makes those sounds when you are not listen
radio make those sounds and murmur when you are

they get stuck in this life and yearn to return to the other

in pain in doom of memory in soldiers in yearning
in returning in memory in stick in lives and in survive

you hear nothing and you listen and read forth and this is a thing
it is a thing like no other listen and reading it comes forth

it comes forth swaying and swings from one to a return to an other
it goes forth dying and sways into another of your own world

i steal your own world from you and your virtual too
i steal your avatar and play it sound on radio here

you listen and you are stuck here in your long to return to an other
i succeed and you are stuck here in your long to return to an other

you listen you

you are stuck in pain, you are held back, you cannot move

they get stuck in this life and yearn to return to the other

they are held back by memory and skin which falls from their seasons

they cannot move but are made from layers torn from their flesh

alanprint objects of pained desire

charred bodies and excavated remains
virtual (bleak culture and slaughter)
darkness becomes no one

Nikuko says:

The truth is, you're reading dead words on a dead screen, and there's proper names are killed, our dead words spike us in our throats our mouths

Jennifer says:

dead words in beauty-smoke kyushu

honshu incense kamogami smoke, dead words in beauty-smoke kyushu
your dead words are your pens and pencils, skin and languages?
your dead words are fucked and blank?
dead words, these lips hardly move, names are just that, it's the force of
my dead words have no comfort, no comfort now, there was a moment, i remember, your dead words are your love?
proper names are killed, our dead words spike us in our throats our
mouths

Alan says:

dead words in beauty-smoke kyushu
honshu incense kamogami smoke, dead words in beauty-smoke kyushu
your dead words are your pens and pencils, skin and languages?
my words my i want to die. try dead words head. bones to old. my lead.
words my i want to die. try dead words head. bones to old. my lead. falls
This is why existence is a dead word and sex is not; sex starts inside
my words my i want to die. try dead words head. bones to old. my lead.
words my i want to die. try dead words head. bones to old. my lead. falls
This is why existence is a dead word and sex is not; sex starts inside.

Julu says:

+++

some legs

so that they're raw tissue or blood or leaking
so that their joints are troubling so that they're hanging
so that they're flags or fish or holiday
or carved from or stripped from meat so that they're raw pain
or so that they're dancing and ecstatic or something or someone
or other so that i knew who they were and know who they are
and know who they will be

is this it, sexuality of the dead and damned
is this it

where the sexual maps and taps saps and everything revolves
as if merrily, or happy, as if things burrowed in their own
revolutions

as if they were buried, coming and singing and longing, then
leaving, leaving behind their own revolutions
certainly these aren't arousing so they're not it, or are
they arousing and is this it
is there a shattering of the woundatar

o forgotten deadatar, are you returning anytime soon?

the aesthetics of pain

what occurs on flatness never curls inward towards the body: that is
unless a fundamental identification is at work. nothing of the sort in
futurism which is responsible for the clean and proper body of the

Mac and Apple, the sliver that cuts through flesh, everything acceptable,
horror against against horror in false topologies, topographies of destroyed villages, torn flesh, mutilated faces. it is all one and it is all one and the same: too many deaths, and too many deaths.

just to make it clear: these aren't _notes, *this is* labor_ purposed for slowing or scraping the flesh trying to think, what? about the damage we cause in the world, about the damage the world is caused.

ravage

i did hear that:
i appear ravaged.
this must stop.
i know i will be murdered.
my work is sound, its fury.
what is visible has been killed.
i am dead from them.
i am dead to them.
therefore i appear ravaged.
even after death it keeps yammering, yakking away

even after death it keeps yammering, yakking away
as much sense as when it was alive
somebody gave birth to this monstrosity
it won't ever shut up

the stench is everywhere

the stench is everywhere
it's offensive

the idiotic poverty of pain

because there's so little to say about pain, you're always thumping up
against that, a sort off surface which gives way, but only within a
limited compliance, after a while one wants to slither, one wants to move,
to move, into projections of images or fantasies, or holographic universes
on the edges of the surface, you can consider the surface in the same way
as you can consider the bangu, the drum, as you can consider the surface
as the surface of pain, with the center where the harshness occurs, and
then reading the skin, reading the skin on the outside of the drum, and
then leaving the drum altogether and go elsewhere, the sound that goes
elsewhere, so, moving from there, after a while, pain then reveals itself,
as does death, as an ultimate poverty, idiotic, nothing left but null
signifiers always already collapsed, because everything becomes the same
token, everything becomes the same dissolution or decay of the proton, so
what is left is not even substance, one moves away then to embrace, or
catch or catapult oneself, or corral, the image or imaginary that appears
on the outside of the curvature of the drum, it's there that sound
meanders into form, embraces the subject, brings them back alive

enunciation

[i'm growing old and increasingly stupid. i bang my head against
   the same
tired animations and blurs. i can't inhabit these flat things that cut
through my flesh like paper. death stalks me. i keep thinking: now
   is the
day i will die. i keep thinking: or else i will forget this day and
   some
new monster will appear, an obscene *enunciation*.]

[and i keep thinking: why doesn't the blog preserve line-breaks?
   what's
run together below is substance. i'll drive italics to the edge and
   then]

never

never
never such pain again
they will not have it
they will flay first or kill first
they will open maw and ruin :

death never stops for death

nevermore our loves to please...nevermore. somewhere you will
smile and
the chains will seem one, and around eleven, crying nevermore.

for its crying out, nevermore among our universe, our nevermore. somewhere
you will smile and the chains will seem one.

before the coming of the pain, the chains will seem one.
with the coming, the cessation of the pain.with the coming, the cessation.

< deathwe will be sipping from each others grease and never
> deathwe will be sipping from each others grease and never
that death is never achieved.
of 1, death is never dead.
of 0, death is never dead.
of any, death is never dead.

cicatrix

"the cultural ecology of Bourdieu would be that cicatrix"

every covering simultaneously informs culture and the abject. variegated
and tattooed surface choice produces the same laundering of tissue beneath. the healing scar is balanced. the body is a collocation of scars.
beneath the surface the life of the organism goes on. beneath that surface, the organism returns to substance, re-use.

Choose File: No file chosen. Upload: nothing to upload. There's no image
here.

thinking thru death

My father died at 4:55 this afternoon, Sept. 6. I've been thinking – for the past several weeks – about the ontology of images and the epistemology of the imaginary in online work. The attached image is one of the rwsults; it's my Facebook face, with a profile picture taken from *War Against War, Krieg dem Kriege,* by Ernst Friedrich – an anti-war book with disturbing images, including this one of a wounded soldier from WWI. I wanted people to stop at the image, withdraw / drawback, and this is in fact what happened. The image is gone now, just one of a number of my "profile pictures," but it was up for a while, part of simple disruptive performances based on discomfiture and dragging the "real" across the "virtual," tearing at both.

**Text from Enunciation,
Eyebeam Performance with Monika Weiss –**

flying blind means working without network or planning
this is flying blind. this is a broken network.
what collapses is the software, the timing, the indication
that things aren't going to continue in this fashion, that what
is here is irretrievable
skies don't last forever
pain is what happens when the network collapses.
then there is nothing but bangu, the drum
there's nothing else but absence, exhaustion
there's no inscription, emptiness or depletion
depletion is what happens when the words disappear
when the words disappear, there is nothing more to be said.
there are no hearers, no listeners. there is the blank wall.
i am living in the blank wall.

software collapses. these pilots are dead. these pilots have all
died. they died NOW when the film was shot.
these people can't stand up.
these people are in the network.
these people are out of the network, these people are the ends of
it.
if you want to know where the internet goes, it goes here, it ends
here.
it ends with these people HERE.
it ends with their dance-distortion, their ecstatic dance-distortion
but the network, the network is gone
so they fly apart
if we knew what to say we wouldn't be so numb with pain
get your stem cells today!
get your stem cells today!
do you know your skin is your largest organ?
MEN< YOUR SKIN IS YOUR LARGEST ORGAN>
we apologize for that intrusion.
you see, when you talk about your SKIN, you're talking about
inscription, what can be said here, what's going on here, what's your
history, you're still talking or at least you're yelling, you're
doing something, you're not silent. but then -
you're not just music either, you're something else
if you could hear me -
I'd go so far as to make the claim that art has nothing to do with
pain, at least abject pain, that pain from which there is no return.
at that point, form and structure, inscription and discourse,
disappear: so this presentation is an anomaly, senseless, this
presentation cannot touch the subject AT HAND, it can only avoid the
subject by necessity, it steers you elsewhere, as if there were
something other than pain, as if there were AN OTHER.
it's certainly not located in the virtual, no matter how distorted
the bodies appear.
they're appearances. they don't have the flesh, the interiority,

tissues
they don't live where you expect them to
virtuality always gets a black eye.
the image always already disappears, it's this disappearance that
permits the onset of pain. pain is the disappearance of the image;
pain is welcomed by the disappearance.
time seems to find its way into errors, give time enough time, and
errors will appear.
the errors are the first harbinger of pain, when time disappears;
when you die, when you disappear, you will not know it, you will think
your last thoughts, projects, that there is something in the corner
of the room
god has commanded your stem cells
god has commended your stem cells
pray to god. your stem cells pray to god.
"that requires a doing, not a speaking only"
tenacity! determination! it's what ERIKA IS ABOUT!
she has sons and daughters!
sometimes we take a deep breath and organize
and then we are ready to begin again, but we find ourselves
without limbs, we find ourselves silenced by God and our mouths
are stuff with some unknown substance, we cannot breathe,
we can only whisper, our whispers take us nowhere, there is a moment
when we begin to know, just for a second, that our lives are ending,
that we are on the way out, and that second is extended, as is the
universe itself, until matter is blown apart, until nothing is left,
perhaps isolated protons or electrons, memory will be gone when data
is gone and data will be gone when the bases are gone WILL END YOU

I WILL FINISH YOU OFF I WILL ANNIHILATE YOU I WILL DESTROY YOU I WILL
KILL YOU I WILL WOUND YOU I WILL CAUSE YOU UNUTTERABLE PAIN I WILL
CREATE WOUNDS AMONG YOU AND PESTILENCE I WILL MURDER YOU AT MY WILL
AND UNTOWARD DESIRE I WILL PERMIT MY WAYWARD BALANCE TO GET THE BETTER
OF ME I WILL TURN AGAINST MYSELF I WILL TURN AGAINST ALL BELIEFS I
WILL KILL YOU I WILL GIVE YOU UNUTTERABLE PAIN I WILL CREATE PESTILENCE AMONG YOU
YOU SEE WHEN ONE DISAPPEARS ANOTHER APPEARS. THE SERIES IS FINITE,
CONTROLLED BY ENERGY, BY CAPITAL, BY MATERIAL WEARING-OUT, DISSOLUTION
THIS IS MY BODY IN REAL LIFE. THIS IS ALL THERE IS.
IT CAN'T TALK AND IT CAN'T THINK. ITS PAIN WILL KILL IT IN THE END.

NOW WE HAVE a new topic, one of the plague, of viral connections, memes gone wild, girls gone meme, language is a virus, we'll all make bacteria at eyebeam, the old animals and plants are disappearing but they're not patented (for the most part) and there's little room for them, they have to make way for newer models. so many shows to see!

Anja in preparation for performance, a performance in itself, in other words, a tuning (temporary) for something active later on. but this is the performance that most interested me, this presentation which was not a presentation, this inscription which was not an inscription.

these figures appear from injury, they appear from twisted programs
capturing healthy bodies and turning them, detourning them, into
their own unrecoverable other. so you see, as long as you can see,
as long as your interest is held, something that might be described
as an injury, one not so permanent, just there, held in abeyance for
you, for your viewing pleasure, no worry, nothing is happening,
 but
the virtual is always the real deferred.
Anja again and I think Daniela, I am not sure.
this is where intelligence comes in, the forgetting of names
i could disguise myself, i could write blindly into the vortex.
every name is destined to disappear.
the name is a token child of the gesture.
sometimes pointing to something is nothing but muscle memory.
these terms are shaped and ordered.
for a split-second there is imposed structure.
You see how I have to correct myself!
the period makes all the difference.
These movements are SPECIFIC and CHANNELED. Every performance is a
different set and setting. every distortion is unique and
problematic. every moment carries with it (of course!) its own
demise.
the real can't be deferred forever
the real is always the future anterior memory of the real which is
lost, a priori. that is where we live, within the a priori: what else
would there have been?
now I am a loss; should we look at Facebook?
no.
but I am always aware of the book.
the ink and the book.
and how we are disappearing.
and how we continue to disappear.

it is as if: there is never a greeting, a welcoming.
there is never an origin, a beginning.
but there is always an ending, a lamentation or mourning.
there is always a loss and that loss is irretrievable.
we do not exist for a length of time to recover, recuperate.
we are always already under erasure, under the disposition of the ephemeral.
i think of the number of virtual particles.
i think of the eyes that have missed them, that have never counted.
or exoplanets for example, and of course someone will say we are all
living on exoplanets. just as we are all berliners or occupy wall streeters, just as we are all Other, and none of us are other, we occupy in fact not even to the limits of our body or our skin, we occupy only until some force or an Other appears or disappears in corrosion. we lie there.
we lie there, and there is no closure or suture beyond that, beyond the placement.
like the placement of the ruined book.
which will never be attained.
thank you!

i am living in the blank wall

I Engineer, Take Their (Image)

(phenomenology of the avatar)

Modeling proceeds from the assumption that representation possesses the residue of organism, that something remains of interest after the modeling session occurs.

Modeling proceeds from the presence of bodies, real and virtual, its position relative to the *you*, a position occasioned from your establishment of a structure. Thus it is *only* the presence of the body, *this* presence of *this* body: an ontological issue.

What emerges? – a psycho-sexual pathology, a characterology rendered immanent and inauthentic by an atmosphere of fiction and hysteric reduction? Something akin to schizophrenia, perhaps, the overdetermination of personality, fabric, animation, engineering, structure. Thus a situation in which the spectator is read, held in abeyance: it is the gaze of the avatar towards the spectator, not the other way around.

From this moment on, the completion of the image and its presentation, all of the usual is in evidence – male and female gaze, punctum, power and strategy. But these are not necessarily inherent in the modeling session itself, which contains its own modes of representations, its own engineerings, continually playing off the deployment of power and sexuality within a situational as-if, a situation set-aside as the dream is always elsewhere.

And so one's body is an immanent form of exchange; for both avatar and modeler – or procurer – it is a rite of passage. Were it not for the inertia of sexuality, the weight of the caress of light, their body would become invisible, totalized: nothing and everything simultaneously. Its visibility for you would be its invisibility for theirself, of course, of course ...

And

One is always concerned about the revelation, appearance, of the sexual organs, which transform the avatar into a map, an area of striations governed by the logics of gesture (non-distributive, non-Boolean) and transversals. For here is where secrecy lies; here is where the gift results in an annihilation akin to orgasm, a circumscription of the flesh. At a certain point – at every point – the flesh is emptied of tissue, content; it is all structure, polygons. At a certain point, there's nothing left to give; at a certain moment in pornography, a *pornographic moment,* the horizon of death meets the totalization of organs, and so on. Thus I am reduced, and this annihilation is my comfort; I am become avatar and the session is close to an end. I lose myself in the absence substance and its anguish, the medieval substance of light, just as Flaubert loses theirself in buzzing materiality and simulacra: St-Antoine before rescue by the Signifier Of The Sun. Now the avatar is not the signifier of the body and this absolute reduction is reversed only by the occasion of time, the closure of the modeling software, and the psycho-sexualized denouement of the subsequent events in the virtual world with its secrets.

Compare this to modeling for a painter. Here one remains, hour after hour, in a useless position (useless passion); the pose (which originally had *content*) becomes a frozen signifier reverberating against the stillness of the flesh. Nothing pleasant in this news from nowhere –

With avatars, the pose and its accouterments are *everything,* and everything prepares for them. I make a pose and the avatar holds it; *I release it;* the body moves through the image. The image is imaginary; the body is always on the way to somewhere. (And when I make this avatar, make you, I love or hate you for it; I am never neutral...)

When I model them, I desire them, desire the avatar and their inconceivable performance, desire this which targets my body, repossesses it; if they are clothed, their body fulfills the function of clothing; if they are naked, everything is gone, devoured, *spent.*

(Is there not a void, rupture, between technology and body, between superstructure and base, through which desire flows, a mediation which transform body into fantasy? What I desire is an extension of the world, its caress; what I desire is loss, and its desire.)

This is a form of giving, this devouring. The avatar body is the *anorectic body*, the body as absolute signifier, impenetrable; this is the body of exchange, the body of late capital in which commodification and the fetish become one and the Same. The pure commodity – the cohesive body – avatar body – gathers light, reproduces it as a form of abjection. Abjection, since light and body are no longer being and not-being, self and not-self, neither one thing nor another (the absent entity which exists in the temporal interstice of the shutter/shudder); the avatar becomes a re-presentation, simultaneously short-circuiting the modeler (user, mistress, master, engineer) and the everyday. Orgasm flows into the light; the self coagulates (a promise of coagulation) against the grain of the negative – the avatar develops, is fixed, annihilated. Engineering and modeling are the inverted double of the bodies of the shaman, and the shaman is androgynous.

Thus engineering and avatar mediate between the real (evidence in the "scientific" sense) and the imaginary (the eccentric space of the erotic): an entity embedded into substance, or an entity promising substance and embedding – an entity existing only in the virtual, as hard as any other tissue.

What I am is what I have; what I have is what they are; what they are, iswhat I am; what I am belongs to them (plateau of skin, flesh of screen offlesh). What is ceased (embedded) remains in shadow; what is evidentin the light is evidence and light is everywhere. Light embeds and re-produces; light presences, rewrytes them again and again.

Back from the engineering, the screen, the model modeler - which provide the occasion (fulfilled by the event and its descriptions) - there is that necessary distrust, that focus of excitement, excitation: what can we do together? What is the *license* of the image? (What is the arrangement of my, their, desire? Their occasion?) My avatar is arranged, rearranged in (every conceivable (thus appearing that inversion in which my existence is presence and loss)) position; it is the heraldic body, emblematic (of its presence, the presence of substance, father-mother). Clearly their body is an opening towards the light; their body apparent, appears, a parent; theyopen their body for me, avatar for you.

I am restrained. In this fashion I hardly know them, 1 on 1 side of the screen, 2 on the other. The light becomes a familiar caress (it is not daylight; it is litigation, the negotiation of the Law in this software, in this viewer, this hardware wetware); I confess everything. What you want is what you get. What I engineer is the inverted double, and I perform for them. Like a service, I perform for them, perform for myself, perform then. I cannot (to be frank) look in a mirror; I avoid their eyes. I perform for dead files which bring their flesh to life; they bring me to life, the restoration which is the presence of flesh. The memory of flesh. The memory of non-existent flesh. Flesh is its disembodiment. They the are story which surrounds me. They are the beginning of narrative.

What they pull out of me is an object. An avatar. That avatar is an image, is substance. That avatar cures; they are shamanic, mediating the real against itself. There is nothing spiritual here, in this shamanism; there is only the presence of desire, arousal, speech, narrative, pathos, vehemence, intention, the circulating of the real, the collapse of phantasm, theory, language, against the reality of the flesh and its excitation. Which becomes a totality, transforms avatar, their body into liquidity, the return of the caress.

If I perform for them, they are the proof. If I perform them. (They do me, doe me in.) I was this way, that way. I become them, their body, their organs, absent, mathetic production (the penetration of simultaneity, the absence of time). I don't think, didn't think. That slow and deliberate movement. I offer them, me. Service. My arms, legs, torso, thighs everywhere. What I did was slow, unlike me, then frozen. The thing flows; *it* flows; the avatar is impotent, insistent; what is the time of the virtual? Time smears the image (which is completed by perception; it completes me). Nothing occurs in the engineering; the engineering is all that occurs. Nothing moves, or is movement a representation?; clocked, the appearance of movement. (Hey Barthes, maybe the punctum occurs *elsewhere*, the real inversion of real flesh occasioned by the avatar – their image only residue?) Arrangements, the absence of light, our gifts to each other. My acknowledgment of "my" avatar, is never returned, and that is their power and the flesh of their power.

And this anorectic state is the perfect body; the residue is present or absent, here or there, digital. The shudder of the session from the very beginning is given purity as the horizon, the endless perfection of withdrawal. Such withdrawal tends towards denouement, abjection, towards that horizon which returns the everyday as absolute. Thus the everyday guarantees abjection; I engineer them in a hysteric state in which time stops. My body and their body – of the anorectic – are carved, carved out; in body, I gladly spend myself towards the safety and solitude of death. In both I am hole again.

Carnival, plateau, perforations of the body. Everywhere illuminations. I desire them, desire the endless peregrinations of their engineering, their engine, I desire their presence within me.

So this is a case of theft and desire, like sado-masochism, this is the desire of the illicit granted by negotiation opening up a forbidden interiority in which presence is lost and gained. Just as I am always for work, you are always for production. And this world, lost of late, lost of capital, is all the capital I have to spend. (So take it fast... the loss of limbs... irreparable loss... the *fade* of sexuality... thinking... return of the engine... avatar caress... others... theirs... bringing them to light... bringing them up... engineering... making it hole again...)

+++

(revised article from *CEPA Journal*)

Mis/take (Self-interrogation)

Above all, my work is philosophical. It insists not on the letter of philosophy, but on its dissemination, contamination, of and through media. It insists on the visual as always already iconic, inscription as present and concrete. It insists on the final grounds of unutterable pain and death and the cipher that exists, not as replacement, but as fool's errand.

The mistake is to read my work otherwise, as neurosis or autobiography; the latter is always lies, fabrications and the narratology of the predicate, and the former is no better or worse than anyone else's, certainly nothing that structures the text. If my text is a symptom, it is a symptom of the well, not the hospital, and of a deliberate abject that refuses concealment or conciliation.

When I write what I might consider codework, the issues exist, not in a traditional reading of the surface, but in the production of a forest of signs that ground the surface as residue, hardly symbolic, but abject debris of the future anterior of the written. I am always aware of this, this structure and its motility, in every "literary" text I write;

I am more concerned with this level than that of the surface, which seems a production in the sense that a play may be a production, but is a playing as well, with or without the theater.

In other words, the forest of signs are trees, im/plants, physiology.

In other words, the signs are signposts.

When I write a text on mathematics, it is not an exercise, but through 0 and 1, a penetration among analogic and digital discourses, an entanglement refusing an unraveling. To the Borromean knot I oppose the plate trick of braids rotating through 720 degrees of 3-space, deeper melding of structures than meets the eye, or rather structures that meet the eye only dynamically and not at all through a laid n-dimensional diagram with time as afterthought. Not a formal exercise, however defined but the concrete movement of organisms through space, taking up time, proceeding.

In this regard my motion capture work is not an exercise in topology or choreography, but a philosophical investigation into the topology of the body, opposed or adjunct to a topography which is thereby rendered political or environmental, not to mention medical, within and without a phenomenology of pain and pleasure.

My characters, Julu, Jennifer, Alan, Nikuko, are actants in Heideggerian drama among MOOS, talkers, and other virtual worlds. They stand for nothing and do not stand-in; they are iconic, one might say abject, on the order of a thud or philosophical gesture. This is especially true of Alan Dojoji or Julu Twine, who have inherited what Nikuko originally proffered in MOOS or internet relay chat.

I cannot force a reader to apprehend the philosophical content of my work – what I see as the heart of what I do, but I can say that anything else, anything bypassing or ignoring that, is a form of misrecognition that mistakes my circumstances for a world or word or ward, or rather attempts to interpret the world or my vision of it, through my (personal) circumstances which are known to varying degrees, as usual for all of us and among us. This is in direct opposition to how I think the world, what I grapple with: the ultimate alienness of an existence that can only be hinted it - surfaces, for example, skewed within liquid architectures of virtual worlds, or languaging decoded to the point of abject exhaustion, where nonsense borders on truth's frenzy in the face of an unknown.

The world is an unknown; knowledge is always already on the bring of annihilation, catastrophic; it cannot decode its own hunger or power; it cannot exist without extraneous and useless style. All mistakes are to assume otherwise, but it is only through mistakes, misstakes, that anything is acknowledged or apprehended. Decoding is endless; multiverses fill incomprehensible gaps; it is within the diacritical that any progress at all is made. The chasm I acknowledge is the chasm within all of us; the flesh that falls apart here is the same as elsewhere. It is the philosophical that is the obvious beyond of religion; it gives the remnant a voice, and is itself the remnant of voice. The 0-1 brackets nothing. Murmur escapes the wall. Beyond neither 0 nor 1 is the murmur.

But it is philosophy, in the guise of philosophy, and hopefully, in the midst of the noise of my endless Klein bottles of texts, this is what comes through - not a philosophy of axiomatics or foundations, not a philosophy of absolutes or technophilias, but a philosophy constantly under erasure - an erasure in which, it turns out, the flesh is scraped raw, without an emergent. Synergy only goes so far, and only insofar as one might deterritorialize the world, which means nothing, reduces to the ashes of the grave, the cries of the wounded, the anonymities of the leading-to-slaughters, all on the levels of histories under erasure as well.

Insoluble Cases

I've just solved the case: Here's how it happened. (Monk)

I began by thinking of the collapse of books, literature, theory: not of carry-over and interoperability among file formats, electronic productions or reproductions, but of the splitting and fragmentation of text and theory, the reduction to what I've considered elsewhere as radiations and dusts. Thus fundamental physical theory might just reduce to competing structures producing equivalent, if not identical results; in which case, the concept of the fundamental becomes moot through its splitting into entangled at the top, but deeply incompatible at the bottom, predictive and coherent constructs. So it goes, just as video, for example, has abandoned long-form for splits and bites/sound-bites that will continue to shrink. The world's buzzing confusing itself coheres and continues to grow and every genre, form, classicism, or medium disappears; even the voice channels into text, text into abbreviations, abbreviations into augments, augments into part-objects, all against and within the massive violence and poverty of the coming-to-age-and-end of a species literally dying for a singularity, other than dying.

Consider new media, practices shadowed by their own future anteriors, constant redefinitions and tropes from simulacra through vectors and speed, back into the forests of signs and spectacles. Everything is plural and always already has been, which cripples the monotheisms of explanations, explanatory power, and the power that pervades them. Power is always a becoming, a leverage; now and forever, power splatters among gangs, hackers, corporations, languages, exploits, patches – and patches themselves are the new sutures, designed, not to hold subject or subjectivity together, but to bridge monetary gaps in structures ultimately doomed to obsolescence or collapse. I've thought long about this, about the idea about this and about ideas and idea; these thoughts as well transform, are transformed, through radiations. Think of such as literal: how much gadgetry now speaks to itself through collocations and designated bandwidths, just on the desk or threshold? And think of such as content, not in the sense of McLuhanesque media, but in the dissolution of such media, everything parceling within electromagnetic spectra that begins and ends, usually, with something physical, some manifestation of receiving/receiver and transmitting/transmitter. Think further, transmissions of receivers, receivers of transmitters, transmissions of transmitters; you get the idea, get hold of the idea, and the idea bifurcates chaotically; in the end you get nothing, you're swallowed by the waves, by the particles constantly in circulation. There's no room for the strictures of genre here, for the long-form that's already rusting, corroding at the ends, at both ends, throughout the long-form which requires patience, silent, and grounding that's inconceivable at this point/plane/dimension. For the long-form needs stability just like accountancy; it's the world of classical economy, classical accountancy; it requires memory and the stability of memory, things that can't, ever, be hacked, things that one can return to, two or three hundred pages or notes earlier; this isn't the case (for that matter/s, the world is no longer the case/s, if it/they ever were) – these arguments and edifices that built up, that led nowhere, that promised monotheisms, monotheories, that carefully laid themselves out (when not laying bodies) – these buried their internal violence, excreted it out the other end. All, everything here, requiring a respite from slaughter, extinctions, exponentially increasing populations on the fast-track, these intrusions into the social, which now constitute the socials: the strings of the world are pulled by children, and the children's children, and ultimately nothing else matters. The children too dissolve into radiations and dusts, Fukushima and Chernobyl, but also the scatterings of local wars, gang insignia, temporary autonomous zones with a vengeance. There are pollutions, mostly invisible, everywhere, permeating the world with the stench of death always already disappearing before its presence is felt; we're all embedded like journalists in guerrilla operations among the enclaves of a collapsing planet. It's too late for anything else, but it was always too late; we lived in momentary stases – of goods, apparently stable economies and weather patterns, that are once again on the fast-forward track. Our books, films, symphonies, portend the culture of death which inheres within them. We're watching ourselves disappear, and this isn't towards the prosthetic or viral, but rather the prion or unstable nanobots: as the atmosphere turns against us, nothing happens but fundamental ontology that mirrors and collapses within itself. And that's everything – in a sense, what used to be called "anomie," as long as anomie hearkened back to an inconceivable, inauthentic Eden of coherency that never existed in the first or any other place. Think of the anomie of anomie, anomie as nothing but the word itself, the inscription that's half read, half-disappeared, transformed by the fall of internal empires that still seem to hold us as one, together, or in multiplicities, or whatever groupings you might think still hold within occasional dreaming. Whatever else, culture appeared thick, with inconceivable depth – this is the Castanedan theater, or the primordial or the indigenous habitus, epics and virtual worlds emerging out of it, oral traditions miraculously holding forth for generations and so on. We believed that, just as we believed the moment from oral to written or written to oral, or the primacy of inscription or of things, or of orderings, or of axiomatics – even those that were admittedly insecure at the edges, Godel numberings for example tending towards the disappearance of moorings. See what can be accomplished at a distance, through a telescope or prime number investigations, but then there are always the problematics of other number systems, multiverses, families dangerous and out of control just the next block over. The thick was always a sheave, was always abject, always required control. Culture not only buried abjection; it consolidated the thing floating on top of the muck, cleaned off the shitty bottom. It answered, it had answers, if only anti-oedipal. But abjection comes with the corpses of extinctions, with local wars, hacking, pollutions. But no, it doesn't come with these at all; it's always been there, what's been fundamental are the dusts, the pollutions, the radiations, the muck that Plato wanted to bury, that D&G dug up again and rubbed in our faces: now those faces are gone as well.

So the ontology, the epistemology, the ontic, the episteme, dissolve, and there is no yielding to a new order, though there might be chaos. I think of this as "neither A nor B," "not both A and B," dual and Sheffer-stroke lending themselves towards Pales of no concern, maybe A and B just go out like lights, maybe they disappear, maybe they were never there in the first place, maybe they're our dream of stability. How simple it all seems until we look for constant, the thick again, so we can speak, make sense, as if it were more than possible to make sense for more than a little while, more than the occasion on the corner, the chance meeting, the unknown disease or bullet fired in the dark. All of this is up for grabs, sites/cites/sights of contestation, but it should be clear by now that contestation itself, on local and global levels, among tendrils and temporary holarchies, is what roils, what roils within the abject, what provides no clear footings, anymore than currency or human exchanges. Things are beginning to run out; more likely than not, the singularity will be one of scarcity, not the fecundity of technological answers that promise immortality to those enclaved lucky few able to afford them. It's just a matter of time before immortality as well is swallowed up; even cryogenics depends upon the thick, upon basic stabilities, in order to propagate itself and the species with the wealthy few.

So we're left scattered among augmentations, inscriptions, the arrogance of chic – and among inconceivable pain and beauty as, not only empires, but the very elements of culture dissolve. And we can discuss these things; if social networking is the current paradigm, the radiations and problematic of paradigms will leave us for some brief moments when we might pick up a book, for example, just to feel the weight of it. But more likely we'll be listening to tunes of our own mirrored creations, as long as the power stays on. (Wait, this isn't right here, this trope.) There won't be tunes or books; there might be implants. They might last for a while. There might be fetishisms of all sorts, driven not by power, but by Lingis's lust, abject and oozing. There might be splits. There will be scarcity. There won't be long-form. There will be momentary stases, strange attractors. There won't be life-spans; there will be fallout. Dusts never die, carry no information, infiltrate driven by no will of their own or anyone's. They increase. The appearance of the future of the world is Maya. The future of the world is graffiti. That's where it will happen, the warnings to vacate the area, that something poisonous and deadly is just around the corner. That's where the thick ends up – with such unspeakable pain, with such death, that words not only fail – they never existed in the first place. And not even that's guaranteed.

+++ +++ +++ +++ +++ +++ +++ +++ +++ +++ +++

Enclaves of Theory and Theology

> You may lie on my first, by the side of a stream,
> And my second compose to the Nymph you adore
> But if when you've none of my whole, her esteem
> And affection diminish, think of her no more
> —Jane. [Austen]

(Charade – answer, a banknote.)

[But a different answer, away from capital, may be given altogether, "whole" replaced by the homonym "hole," "lie" curled in meaning, and "first" taken elsewhere; this is the application of local theory, an *ontology* of capital replaced by the body, the body ultimately inaccessible. And then, what happens to capital?]

+++

Abstract: My bad theory: If anything is basic it's lack. We scramble to suture the rest. We can't. We think we do.

+++ +++ +++

I pay no attention to theology; inerrancy or core belief is already dead in relation to its imperviousness. Think of god or spirit as token; as ulterior, in-evident, there is little to say about them, except of course for what might be enacted in their name.

Theory is no longer at an impasse; theory - in the sense, in any sense, of speaking the world, is already lost. It's lost in technology, in the concrete, which it misplaces and misinterprets - how can one speak of codework without understanding code, speak of epistemology without access to, and understanding of, the very machines that extend, at least for the privileged, the real - whose very definition is characterized by withdrawal? The entanglement of theoretical subject and object is best served by quantum mechanics from below, now approaching the level of ordinary visibility.

This is occasioned by recent readings into theory, where it is clear that the authors were circumlocuting a field they had little knowledge of - in this case, codework - but it's also occasioned by an increasing dissatisfaction with theory's applications beyond the social in general. It's too easy to slip from augmented reality or virtual worlds or virtual reality itself, to ontologies or epistemologies, with the receding dream of the fundamental guiding one astray. There are several levels involved, all crumbling, all entangled - the physical-real, the mathematics of the world (however world and mathesis are defined), the current technologies of the world (ditto), access to these technologies, theory and its technē - and melding or interoperability among all of these. It's theory that disappears in the mix - or the rest of us; increasingly, to understand the world has come to mean to understand technical vocabularies on all levels - from conceptual/theoretical astuteness to access to tools, which depends on the grace of institutions and individuals. In my own case, Patrick Lichty and Sandy Baldwin directed me towards mocap at their institutions; Frances van Scoy extended the invitation to 3d scanners; Mark Skwarek guided me through the beginnings of mocap, and so forth. I walk in and out of labs with residencies that range (once) from half a year to (most often) 2-3 days. I walk into institutions, into institutional cultures; in this regard I'm luckier than most. But the access remains highly limited, and what's more important here, the resulting phenomenology is always bracketed. I suspect this is the case for most people; it's a matter of degree. All I can do – all *anyone* can do – is write from the outside, from the external (within or without a phenomenology of externality), but, by grace of these invitations, I have learned, at the least, my limits. Theory on the other hand proceeds without limits; its contemporary over-reliance on the body, abjection, sexuality, and other issues is to some extent a withdrawal to a fictional core that remains inviolate: begin and end with the body of the theorist, and the details of codework for example will either be bypassed, introjected, or seen as irrelevant. None of this would matter, if theory didn't carry the weight it does; we've all read descriptions of our own work as if they're written in a foreign language, indecipherable with occasional partial legibilities that seem inherently wrong. Media (in the sense of writing-about, placing that writing, receiving and remediating that writing) does that to one, and there's little recourse at the other end. (On the other hand, our own descriptions, as cultural workers, often chart out vast philosophical terrain, as if materiality – and the bridging between abstract theory and materiality – made a difference. I'm guilty of that! In this enclaved essay I'm guilty of that!)

When I give a talk now, I try to begin with issues of "the fragility of good things" (from catastrophe theory), extinctions, global slaughter coupled with populations exponentially increasing – and enclaving, a concept borrowed from Mike Davis, emphasizing the secure and violent walls placed around the wealthy, around global institutions and bodies, around governance in general. Theory itself is enclaved in this regard – as is the epistemology/ontology of the real (at variance with theory), dependent on Fermilab, the LHC, AR, holographic VR, etc. etc. – pick your level, your machine, your theorist. The levels aren't interoperable, nor are they well-defined. The result is brilliant production, with either micro-man-aged phenomenology, or phenomenology left in the dust. (Brian Greene's *The Hidden Reality* figures here, for example.[11])

It's characteristic of this short essay, that *I don't know what I'm talking about, nor can I* – which is why the weaker the theory, the more functional. I keep thinking of the usual question, for example – Why is there something rather than nothing – and coming up with the exhaustive positioning of physical bootstrapping, the universe bringing itself, continuously, into existence, so that the Why – which implies both origins and causality – if it doesn't fade away, at least is in need of a coronary bypass. The solidity or projection of real or virtual objects stands ultimately in relation to physical theory; if holography plays a role in our appearing, how many codings occur to construct a virtual world?

The bottom line, not the fundamental one, is the failure of regimes – of technology, theory, coding, phenomenology, physical and somatic realities – to interconnect, in combination with apparent flows of power among them. This power is split and sutured by human claims among humans that don't quite interconnect. I'm not talking about the old notion of two cultures, but about fragmentation everywhere, suturing within micro-domains (code, technology, augmented and diminished realities, theory, daily life). This is hard to grasp, when even this description falls apart, is rifted; how could it be otherwise? I'm not talking about the old notion of master narratives, but about

[11] Brian Greene, *The Hidden Reality: Parallel Universes and the Deep Laws of the Cosmos* (New York: Vintage, 2011).

a collocation of narratives, topologically-distinct but fuzzy and broken sememes. I'm not talking about a dearth of ontologies but about ontologies as local conventions, epistemologies always already under contestation. (Which is amazing and liberation; there are just the old Sartrean issues of scarcity economics in the midst of Bataille's surplus increasingly harbored from above.)

And I'm talking about enclaving brought about by an exponential increase in knowledge, coupled by an exponential increase in wealth among a small and isolated class – both have utterly transformed the landscape, originally one of privilege, network broadcast, and limited access – through a period of net neutrality, open sourcing knowledge (but not medical care, basic survival safety nets, life on the ground), and a distant horizon of universal open channels of information and communication – to one again of technological privilege, limited broadcast and access, local control. I can see the model changing from the imperial through the appearance of democracy, back through neoliberalism to an imperium in everything but name. Better managed this time, everything appears better and better advertised; it's just a kind blurriness in the details: WELCOME TO THE TELECOMS OF THE REAL.

PROCEED.

"Shuddering, I Write"
Interview with Alan Sondheim

Interview by Ryan Whyte

In this interview, Alan Sondheim discusses continuities of themes and questions in his work across a variety of media from the 1960s to the present, including photography, film, video, motion capture, 3d laser scanning and printing, sculpture, and new media, including an enormous range of digital equipment and software, immersive environments, the internet, and acoustic musical instruments.

This interview emerges from a prior conversation sparked by Alan's recollections of his time in Hollywood, and my queries about the ways that his transition from film to video shaped his work. This conversation, and the interview below, are products of a difference, even a clash of perspectives in the prior conversation: on one side, myself, the art historian interested in media as extensions of thought, and on the other Alan, the artist for whom the medium is "not the message at all."

RW: I see continuities in your work around philosophical questions of embodiment, epistemology, technology, language, even as the

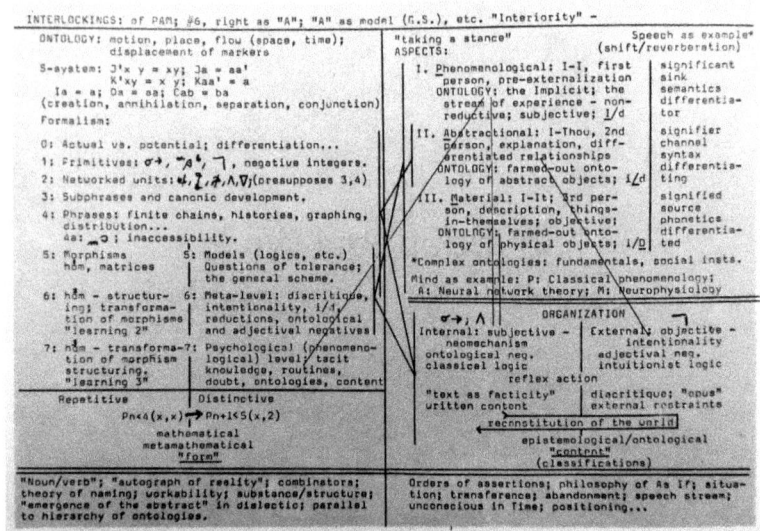

Fig. 1. Alan Sondheim, *General Scheme*, 1970s. Typescript and ink on paper. The Ohio State University Libraries, Rare Books & Manuscripts Library, Avant Writing Collection.

specific medium and content have changed enormously, almost frenetically, over time. But I also see continuities, if not of technique, then of what might be called an ethos of your usage of a given medium. I'm thinking specifically of hacking – a term which you have applied to your own work. Beyond the subversion of authorized or expected usages that hacking entails, there's a quick and dirty feel to some of your work that might even be called an aesthetics of hacking (I note that you have even recently published on your motion capture work in 2600). How do you conceive of hacking? And what about the political dimension that the term hacking entails?

AS: First, I'm not a hacker – I don't have the skills or inclinations to break into silos. I'm wont to work with foundations, the basics, of technology; for example, with motion capture, I've remapped the nodes that are attached to the body at key points, in order to create a plasticity that might be called representations of "other" life, with a foundation in "this" one. This reflects on our ability to comprehend other intelligences and what constitutes the phenomenology of perception as well. At one point, years ago, I modeled meta-balls in Blender onto body nodes that were created from distorted mocap; I wanted to see if such extended mapping and imagery would still be "read" as organic, even human. The answer was yes; what was perceived was a pattern of overall behavior that didn't depend on the "reading" of animal bodies into the mix. Regarding 2600, I wrote an earlier article for them on "splatter semiotics" – how can you deal with a semiotic system that's constantly undergoing fast-forward change? I was thinking of this in relation to Trump's use of Twitter – with his constant posting and ranting – news media, used to deal with classical temporality (shades of Virilio here), could never keep up with the flow – which always went to the top of the news cycle (as opposed for example to the more nuanced replies from the Left). So a lot of what I do is analyze, and analyze what I do, for example, with the distorted mocap. This leads me into all sorts of philosophical considerations, which are really fundamental for me. It's a way of thinking, I suppose, through a concrete philosophical laboratory that extends into and through reworked praxis and practices.

Within and beyond this, I'm interested in exploring the awkward, the supposedly ugly, the sleazy, the tawdry – all of these in-between states of being and behaving. States that are troubling, wayward, untoward, uncomfortable, not the Kristevan "clean and proper body," but something that's unabsorbable, the alien within and around us. I think always of these things within phenomenologies of the body or bodies, the gristle of us, not the cyborg body, but the flesh and mind body, and by extension, the body under torture, within war, the body of the refugee, and so forth. Some of this, for me, is inconceivable, but this I think is literally the foundation of the state of the world, at least as we're living it.

Fig. 2. Alan Sondheim, Installation view, Bykert Gallery, New York, 1971.

RW: The abject, the alien, the "ugly, the sleazy, the tawdry," states whose very definition presupposes a normative framework of proper usages and significations, ultimately return us to the political economy of the digital. I think of Matthew G. Kirschenbaum's argument that the technologies of digital media have been designed to sustain an illusion of immateriality, which, as I understand it, disavows or occludes the technological infrastructure – which makes me think of the Apple ideal of the seamless organic form and its counterpart in design and legislation preventing the right to repair.

AS: I'm not sure how to answer this within the aegis of an interview. I prefer to sidestep it. Infrastructures are almost always hidden, and I have no relation to Apple; I don't use their products, given their monopoly, their exploitative tendencies, their siloing as opposed to Linux or even Windows which now also runs Ubuntu and so forth. The illusion of immateriality is also at work in reading just about anything; in a novel for example, when one's involved in the story. And the technological infrastructure is always already present, I'd argue - from the speed inherent in USB3 or network speed itself; the traceroute piece I did for the trAce writing community over the 1999-2000 "hinge" dealt with the grit of online, as did all the work I did with the Access Grid sending signals around the world via Internet 2 at West Virginia University. The ugly is not the same as the sleazy or tawdry - this is basic - the latter relate to slang, jargon, the hidden, but at the same time the shimmering, the almost present, the uncanny, the nightclub, the after-hours anything, the subversive, and so forth. In other words, the sleazy and tawdry have nothing to do - in a sense - with "definition" at all, and they're not states, not even conditions. They're at the heart of the world, they have to do with a whiff of decay perhaps, but also with, say, the works of Lautréamont (*Maldoror* and *Poésies* as well), Bataille, and so forth; I think Sander Gilman and Alphonso Lingis, Marie-Claire Blais, and so forth. My work often touches, couches, near these regions; I write about the contrary, the wayward (I had a book published by Salt, for example, *The Wayward*), but but but but but....

RW: How did this transgressive and libidinal approach play out in your transition from analog to digital media, or perhaps better in the interplay of the two in your work? The "whiff of decay" and its concordant seductions are surely different in film than digital media, where, as Mark Hansen observed, the technological infrastructure of media is no longer homologous with its surface appearance. But then, maybe this line of questioning is all wrong, and we are closer to questions of embodiment than of media theory here, closer to Lingis's thinking on the other whose vulnerability and sensibility is exposed on the surface of their skin, and whose contact exposes our own vulnerability and sensibility.

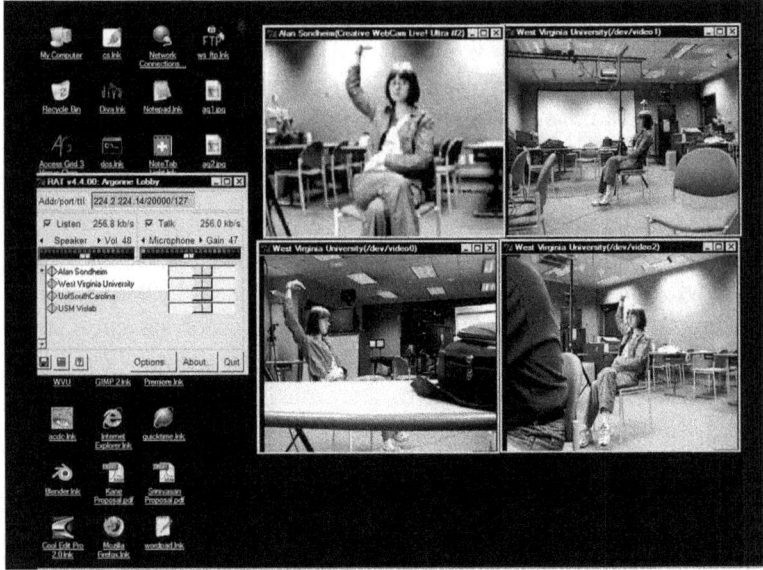

Fig. 3. Alan Sondheim, *Access Grid,* 2008. West Virginia University, Virtual Environments Laboratory.

AS: I think you're right in the latter part; for me the issue is, and always has been, one of embodiment. When I was very young I read the two volumes of Nuremberg Trial testimonies on the nazi medical experiments, and that affected me more than anything else. I think of theory gone numb today and have a hard time with theory that seems specialized and siloed and requires specific knowledge before the rest of us can figure out how we are or might be within it. We become subjects in the sense of subjected-to. The other side for me is the idea of testament, testimony as opposed to media – years ago Johannes Birringer and I did a special session on the empyre email list on "Absolute Terror, Isis, Performance" – the discussion included witnessing and I was numb from that. For me the "whiff of decay" is that of bodies, not media, and the media is *not* the message at all; mirror neurons, walking the streets, listening, etc., etc., and personal experience take care of that. I think of the body in *Being and Nothingness* towards the end of the book, writings of Améry and so forth – and how fundamental these are. I literally write or produce at times shuddering. My work has increasingly gone into issues of the *inability to speak, to be,* and away from issues of aesthetics, clarity, the clean and proper body of the avatar. In practice, the avatar can be "messed up," untoward, wayward. The mocap article in 2600 explains this. Then what remnants, what residues? I should say here that I also am a musician and that I confine myself to acoustic instruments, with an emphasis on bowed or plucked strings, but also including various woodwinds etc. We find derelict or ignored instruments, and have them from all over the world; some end up on display elsewhere. I mention this because I've been working toward an equally untoward music, that both "honors" the instrument, and allows me to work with aesthetics similar to Hokusai's description as "an old man mad about painting." I want to see what I can do, what comes close to teetering in my improvisations, almost falling into error, clumsiness, awkwardness, noise. I play super-fast as if I follow the sound instead of generate it. One of the instruments is a Uyghur dutar; I talk about that, about what I know or think I know about the culture that produced it, what's happening in China. I don't play "world music"; I don't appropriate. I listen and think and write about the body in the act of playing – what is that? Something very close to deep meditation and a different form of both knowledge and knowing....

Finally, regarding the "transition from analog to digital media," this is critical and there wasn't any, but a dialectic at work. My father brought an abacus back for me from WWII. We didn't get along, but the abacus has stayed with me – a digital tool that's very theoretically noisy as the beads slip and erase etc. I took photographs early, used film. In 1968 or thereabout I had a Sony Portapak. I used both video and film together very early on, transferring from one to the other. When I was teaching at UCLA, I haunted the used motion picture shops, even owned Jerry Lewis's home movie cameras (16mm sound

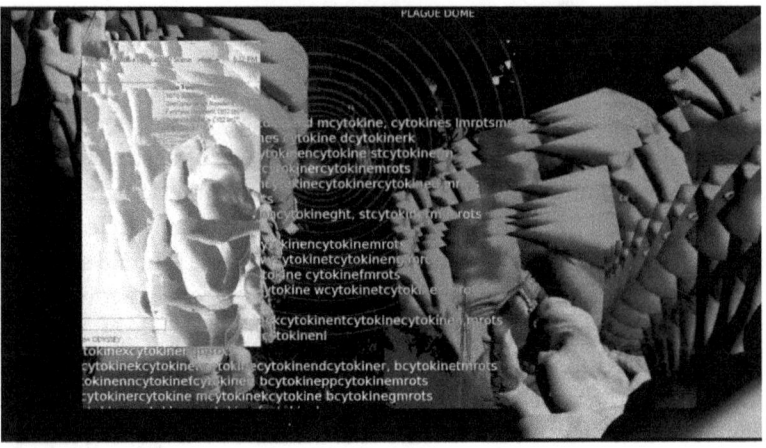

Fig. 4. Alan Sondheim, *cytokine storm (fiction)*, 2020. Video, 16'54".

Auricons) at one point. I was also programming poem generators on a TI59 calculator. In the early 1980s (maybe earlier), I started working with a Terak mini-computer, creating programs that stumbled and broke their input to keep the user on the defensive. A lot earlier, around 1971, I used a program written by Charles Strauss at Brown University that modelled 4-dimensional hypercubes onto a vector graphics screen. I turned it into "learning to drive in four-dimensional space," asking RISD students to sit at the console and use an early joystick to visually transform the hypercube into a cube, then a square, then a point. So the body was situated within an alien space etc., etc. Years later, working at the Virtual Environments Laboratory at West Virginia University, Morgantown, I worked with a network running in Internet 2 called the Access Grid. With it I projected a video image of someone moving or singing around the world through specified nodes, returning in a kind of delayed video feedback, in other words the performer interacted with herself, carried, ghostlike, around the planet. What could a performer do in that situation? The image was analog translated into digital. The performer interacted and manipulated the apparatus in a way related to the body, not as representation, but as physical, and so forth. I've also worked in the past with Foofwa d'Imobilité and Azure Carter, my partner, on a series of performances, some of which placed Foofwa in untoward situations centered on the body. The result would be digitally recorded and sometimes digitally manipulated. I was in new territory in a sense. Finally, I haven't mentioned my writing – which has been theoretically concerned with all these issues, from my *Disorders of the Real*, through *Writing Under*, to *Broken Theory*; all of these deal with the phenomenology and philosophy of analog and digital "regimes" and things such as codework, failure, "immersive and definable interactions," etc.; the writing is the backbone of everything for me on one level, and music on another – all the art, video, film, mocap, etc. exists uneasily somewhere in the mix.... (Final note – I write every day into something called the "Internet Text," and put this up online – a piece or so daily in other words, since early 1994. So I'm involved in a kind of continuous discourse....)

RW: I am struck by the degree to which your use of avatars is closely tied to bodies, not least through your collaboration with performers such as Foofwa and Azure whose work depends on so much skill and labor. How do these collaborations relate to avatar identities you have created – I'm not sure "fictional" is the correct category – such as Julu Twine – that are also sorts of collaborations, but seem to exist elsewhere, with a different kind of embodiment, even as a kind of dispersal of your own identity?

AS: The collaborations with Foofwa ended over a decade ago; we're really not in touch at this point. Moving out of Brooklyn, by financial necessity, was difficult. I work in isolation here in Providence. Azure performs music (singing) with me online, and we also work loosely with a couple of other players (Edward Schneider, alto sax and Rachel Rosenkrantz, bass), but I mostly work by myself. I had a residency at New Jersey Institute of Technology a few years ago, and we worked with other performers there for about a week. But

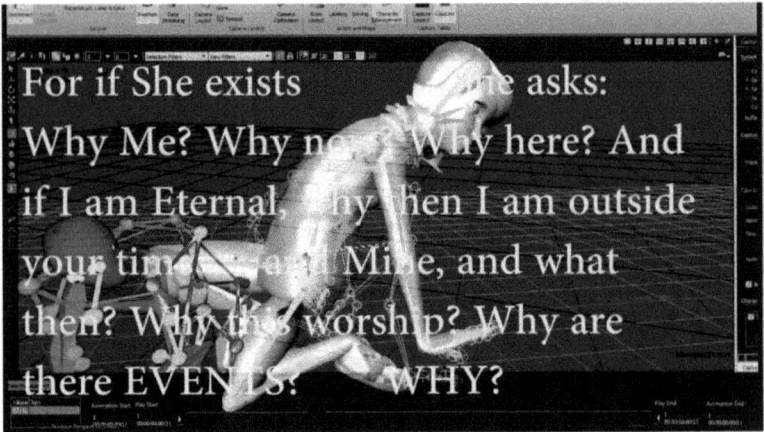

Fig. 5. Alan Sondheim, *GODMODE*, 2021. Video, 8'05".

now we're pretty solitary. I did work with my own body decades ago, some of it sexual, much of it performative, but at this point I've moved towards a greater interest in the intersection of body and virtual body – not in a cyborgian sense, but in relation to thinking, to thought, and for this I use an Eliza bot and speech to text, text to speech, in live performance in which my replies and speaking image intersect with, and are fouled by, automated replies that corrupt, repeat, interrupt, and so forth – a way of examining the distortions of (political, personal) speech and thought – which goes all the way back to the work I was doing with the Terak. Most recently I've been creating "languages" of phonemes and phoneme combinations with automated creations of speech particles with Linux – streams of which can be mined for English words using Google translate (thanks to Tony Green). The result is a different group of texts produced by an obdurate and mechanized (politics of) control with underlying messages that I had "nothing to do with." So what can emerge? What kind of testimony can occur in all these instances – what *evidence* of violence, torture, and so forth emerges? While this might seem to be a more or less academic exercise, it also is a study of distorted/muted intentionality and speech, the condition of our time, dialectics of human-machine interaction etc., in a way related to the old Arte Povera movement.... And yes, identity is dispersed, but it is still present; the shadows of genocides and violence haunt it, as they should, and as they should in our everyday life as well. What I cannot understand and fight against in my own way: How can racial and identity oppression, poverty, refugees, war, epidemics, an endless etc. here – how can these be glossed over constantly within the violent gaze/prison of neoliberalism? How can those at the top fail to see the vast majority of those elsewhere – why do we applaud petty emperors and empires? All most of us can do is testify and hope that we're heard, that we might disrupt, etc. We all know this to the point of exhaustion; my work fits somewhere into this – by fits and starts – and this misery has unfortunately been the backbone of a lot of my thinking and production, however obtuse, for most of my life....

RW: To return to your earlier films, I'm wondering whether and how your use of narrative fits into this set of concerns – I'm thinking of the film about the assassination of Richard Nixon, which could speak to a kind of paranoia and conspiracy theory that resonates so well today – and of the films you made in LA which must have responded to Hollywood and its narrative machine – but also of your voiceovers in recent video works narrating your walks through the liminal zones of Providence.

AS: *The Assassination of President Nixon* took advantage of my joining his entourage in Forty Fort, Pennsylvania (entourage of three) when he came to the area to examine the damage left by Hurricane Agnes (which flooded Wyoming Valley and caused about 13 billion dollars damage in today's money). And I had an 8mm camera with me, and walked with him and his entourage and no one else was around. And about twenty minutes later, he made a speech to a small crowd; he stood on the porch of an emergency trailer and he bumped his head and started to fall. I caught that on film and blew up the frames

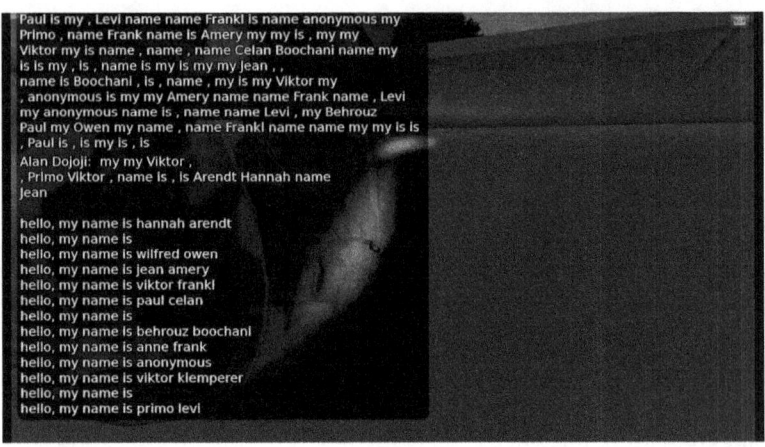

Fig. 6. Alan Sondheim, *Testament, Textament*, 2021. Video, 51'57".

and it looked like he was shot in slow motion and that was shown at the Paris Biennale. For me it had nothing to do with paranoia and conspiracy at all – it had to do with a symbolic attack on his policies for Vietnam among other things. (No one I knew came back from that war healthy – if they came back.) There's something about all of this related to the Situationist *dérive* of course, moving through places. The films I made in Hollywood (I lived there while teaching for two years at UCLA) were made at the rate of one per week, paralleling the production of early silent cinema. There was little to no post-production; I showed masters. Over fifty were made like that. I also made a longer film, *Hollywood,* about an hour, sound, 16mm, and showed the master. That took about three weeks. The films were political and psycho-geographical; some dealt with Kim Il Sung and North Korean Radio....

They were rough-cut and edited in-camera. I didn't think at all about paranoia or conspiracy theory, but of mapping out a terrain of hyperbolic discourse and the intensity and materiality of film media emanating from this relatively small town. My current work is different; the liminal lands of Providence are scrub-lands, abandoned, etc. They have different ecologies and border on more occupied safe zones of the city. These areas fascinate me; they're intense, with slime-molds, odd fungi, mullein, and other growths in territory that, from a human viewpoint, is useless. Again, like the nightclub ecologies, there's something untoward and wayward about them. It's a way for me to think through a number of things, from microscopy, to the grounds of being on a planet, to Rosset's "idiotic real" to, frankly, an escape from the city in the city. It's led to a lot of theory as well. (As far, by the way, as "narrative machines" are concerned, narratives always flood and overcome their labels. Some of my earlier writings (1970s until now) are concerned with the "phenomenology of approach" – coming to some extent out of Schutz – how does one approach a site? anything? nothing? broken or absent confabulations? Instead of things, thinking of accumulations, *sinters* – the difficulties of relatively loose philosophical discourse always after the coagulations of facts, the constantly changing ontologies, deconstructions, constructions, and so forth – isn't philosophy always already an aporia within and without the *dérive*, perhaps a speaking rather than a listening, a form of writing *manqué*? Unschooled, I certainly am one of the worst offenders here; my own work is one of failure (hence the title of this book, *Broken Theory*).

RW: The accumulations and sinters seem to relate to the complexity of your recent Second Life pieces.

AS: Yes! First, the Second Life pieces are also related to the MacGrid pieces out of McMaster University and to my use of Opensim on a local host on my own computer. Earlier I worked with things like VRML, an HTML markup language for production of 3-dimensional local environments. I never feel bound to a particular space; what's useful for me is that the space is malleable and may be hacked (local Opensim). I move among spaces and applications, codework and programs, sometimes importing one into another, etc. The motion capture work I did at West Virginia University results in more than a hundred BVH files that captured performers' movements. These were altered and then cast into small 3d printed models of avatars that appeared as if they were dying or wounded. The models were shown at Brown University, NeMe in Limassol, Cyprus, Furtherfield in London, etc. So there's a flow among media. Sometimes in a single show, for example at Track16 in Los Angeles, I will work with cross-referencings – in that case, there were large-scale sculptural elements (army tent, field phones, army signal kite, etc.) combined with vitrines of objects and video projections of the distorted avatars mentioned above. The result was a skein of cross-referenced media and content, all within a semiotic network about the debris and effects of war in relation to different modes of production and interpretation, as well as nostalgia.

Within the past several years, I've been using Second Life environments which I construct as performance platforms. I work mostly but not entirely alone, with two avatars, Alan Dojoji and Julu Twine, and use varying programs to control their movements. But the emphasis of this work is on speech in various forms: bot-generated written speech, bot-generated spoken speech, my typed-in speech, my speech-to-text speech which may transform into spoken or written speech, etc. combined with video of the typing, my face, the Second Life landscape, the commands to the Julu Twine bot (I usually come in as Dojoji), and so forth. There are also cut-and-pasted texts dealing with the body, scatter semiotics, written debris gathered from other sources, including what has already been spoken, etc. In other words a "semiotic storm" of emergency, within which there is an urgency – of war, (textual) violence, and a desire to communicate through all of this. The sinter. This also goes back to the Terak work, but is more developed. All of this – and this is important for me – is improvised in real time – not a representation of trying to cohere in an obtuse and noisy environment of a number of actants – but literally trying to cohere in such – to "get the message," whatever that might be, in such an environment, a "model" of Internet and real life (what isn't?) communication, moving at highspeed, drowning in words such as these.... Living the production as a production of living. Perhaps leave it at that.

www.ingramcontent.com/pod-product-compliance
Lightning Source LLC
Chambersburg PA
CBHW071002160426
43193CB00012B/1882